D1047285

THE SURVIVOR

THE SURVIVOR

THE TRUE STORY OF THE SINKING
OF THE *DOGGERBANK*

by

HANS HERLIN

Translated by

JOHN BROWNJOHN

LEO COOPER
LONDON

First published in Great Britain in 1994 by
LEO COOPER
190 Shaftesbury Avenue, London WC2H 8JL
an imprint of
Pen & Sword Books Ltd
47 Church Street, Barnsley, South Yorks, S70 2AS

Copyright © Hans Herlin, 1994

Translation copyright © John Brownjohn, 1994

ISBN 0 85052 409 1

PRINTED IN THE U.S.A.

To Boatswain Fritz Kuert,
sole surviving member of
the crew of the Doggerbank,
of whom 364 perished

CONTENTS

FOREWORD

It was in the 1960s, while researching a series of articles about U-boat captains for *Stern* magazine, that I first came across an account of the sinking of the *Doggerbank*. I was so fascinated by this extraordinary but hitherto unpublicized tale of human error and human endurance that I resolved to contact the ship's sole survivor, Fritz Kuert.

I ran him to earth at Lünen, in what was then the British Zone of Germany, living with his wife and three children in the coalminer's cottage where he had been born. He still showed signs of the wartime ordeal that had permanently impaired his health, but his stocky build and steady gaze were those of a man who had once possessed the mental and physical stamina to survive against all odds.

Kuert was not only willing but eager to tell me his story, every detail of which had etched itself into his memory. Indeed, he was so obsessed by the wish to speak out on behalf of his dead shipmates that my shorthand could not cope with his torrent of words and I had to use a tape-recorder.

Although greatly impressed by the man and his obvious sincerity, I took care to verify the information he had given me. I not only examined the transcript of the inquiry into the sinking held at HQ C.-in-C. U-Boats but interviewed surviving members of *U43*'s crew who had left the submarine prior to its final patrol. Thus, every detail of what follows has been either transcribed from Kuert's own tape-recorded account of what was said and done in the course of those fateful twenty-six days in March, 1943, or confirmed by other sources.

Like many German members of that international fraternity, the merchant marine, Fritz Kuert laced his native tongue with a good deal of English, which he spoke and understood quite well. My one regret is that he did not live to see this first English-language edition of his memorable story. He died on 27 July, 1986.

HANS HERLIN

PROLOGUE

The city and lake of Geneva were shrouded in white, vaporous mist on 16 January, 1944.

It had started to snow toward midday, and fat snowflakes were drifting across the railway tracks leading into the Gare du Cornavin. All that could be seen of the name on the station signboard were Geneva's last three letters: '. . . ÈVE'. The hands of the clock were obscured by a coating of snow and ice.

Men and women wearing Red Cross armbands shivered as they stood waiting at two trestle tables, hot coffee steamed in big aluminium pots, Swiss soldiers stamped a little warmth into their feet on the crusty snow. The two prisoner-of-war specials were scheduled to arrive at 3 p.m.

As usual when an exchange of prisoners was to take place, the Red Cross had notified the Swiss military authorities and the German and American consulates. The American POWs had been brought to Constance from camps in various parts of Germany; their German counterparts from the USA had been shipped across the Atlantic in the *Charles A. Stafford* and put aboard a special train at Marseilles.

There was a shrill, piercing whistle in the distance: the train from Constance was approaching. It halted outside the station, a dark line of carriages just visible through the whirling whiteness. Then a wire bordering the tracks went taut, dislodging its burden of snow, and the signal pivoted upwards.

Two men in black, fur-trimmed overcoats identified themselves to the sentries. The Swiss examined the German diplomats' papers politely but coolly before returning them with a look of mingled curiosity and condescension, unable to disguise their belief that the pair were there as representatives of an already defeated nation. The American consular officials had earlier received a far more cordial reception.

The platform vibrated underfoot as the train from Constance pulled in. The tender of the German locomotive bore the regulation Propaganda Ministry slogan – WHEELS MUST TURN FOR VICTORY! – but this had been tactfully painted over for the occasion. The taller of the two Germans, whose cold-reddened cheeks were adorned with duelling scars, said, 'Our own boys should be arriving any time now.'

Doors burst open all along the train and eager figures jumped down on to the platform, filling the air with loud, exuberant American voices. They bent down, made snowballs and pelted each other like children let out of school. The Swiss sentries hustled them back inside and closed the doors again. The women with Red Cross armbands progressed from carriage to carriage with their aluminium coffee pots and cardboard cups.

The man with the duelling scars, which stood out white against his ruddy cheeks, produced a list of German POWs from his sleeve turn-up. It was several sheets long and comprised 417 names. One entry on the third sheet was underlined in red:

Surname Kuert, given names Fritz, Louis, August, Otto; born 7 August 1918; place of birth Lünen, Westphalia; nationality German; rank boatswain; last-known address, PW 2000 NA, Valley Forge PW Camp.

'That's our man. We don't have a personal description, but they'll call the roll. What we need is a decent photograph of him, so get ready with your Leica.'

'Why are they so keen to whisk him back to Germany?' asked the shorter of the two men, who had a camera dangling from his neck. 'Did he shoot his mouth off to the Yanks?'

A dark plume of vapour rose from the locomotive's smokestack. A coupling fell with a crash. The locomotive moved off, two armed sentries on the running boards. 'His ship was sunk,' the man with the duelling scars said tersely. 'He's the sole survivor.'

'What ship was that?'

'The *Doggerbank*.'

The locomotive disappeared into a flurry of snow. Its wheels clattered across a set of points.

'The *Doggerbank*?' The second man looked intrigued. 'Wasn't there a report about her on the Di-di-di-dum?' He meant the BBC's German-language broadcasts, with their V-for-victory call sign. 'Wasn't she the blockade-runner that got sunk by our own people?'

The man with the duelling scars didn't reply. He turned up his fur collar and set off along the train. The carriage windows were filmed with condensation. The wind whipped loose snow off the roofs and dusted the platform with it.

The snow-encrusted train from Marseilles had pulled into the platform alongside. The stretcher cases made their exit first, thickly swathed in blankets. Little puffs of frozen breath issued from their lips as Red Cross attendants carried them over to the train with the misted windows. The American POWs had vacated it and were waiting behind a rope strung across the platform. Silently, the Germans emerged from the Marseilles train and stood in line at one of the tables, where Red Cross officials checked their names on a list.

Two prisoners approached the table. One was thin and pale, with a deeply indented scar in his right temple and the fixed gaze of a blind man. 'Kürzinger,' he said, 'Josef.'

The other man, who was guiding him, wore a strange mishmash of uniforms: a long U-boat greatcoat, a thick white woollen scarf, and the cap of a master in the merchant marine. His face was framed by a luxuriant beard. When he spoke, he displayed five gold teeth. 'Kuert, Fritz,' he said, 'boatswain.' He made a civilian impression in spite of his peculiar uniform.

'Next!'

The man named Kuert led his blind companion over to the train, helped him on to the step, handed him his suitcase.

Once on board, he turned and looked back. One of the men in dark overcoats had raised his camera. He clicked the button, wound the film on, and clicked the button again. Kuert gave an automatic smile, as if he found nothing strange about the scene or the attention bestowed on him. He smiled into the camera and said, 'Do I get a copy?'

Many years later he would receive an anonymous letter – or rather, an envelope that gave no hint of the sender's address. It contained a print of one of the photographs, nothing more. Just a snapshot with a simple inscription on the back: *Gare du Cornavin, 16 January 1944.*

The men in the fur-trimmed overcoats headed for the exit. Names were still being called out behind them. A railwayman was making his way along the platform, freeing frozen brake shoes with a long-handled hammer.

'Well?' said the man with the duelling scars.

'He didn't seem to mind being photographed. He actually smiled for the camera.'

Outside in the Place du Cornavin their driver was waiting for them beside a car with CD plates. Newspaper sellers were shouting the headlines of the evening editions. The Germans' faces turned to stone.

'Red Army breakthrough on the Vistula!'

'German Ardennes offensive halted!'

The two diplomats sat stiffly in the back of the car. They didn't look at each other, merely stared out at Geneva's broad, brightly-lit streets.

Just as their car turned into the rue de Mont Blanc, the German train's long line of carriages left the station and disappeared into the murk.

The man in the submariner's greatcoat and his blind companion were installed in window seats. The lake made a brief appearance, wreathed in mist.

'The lake's on our left,' Kuert said. 'Looks like grey soup. You can hardly see a thing.' He'd grown accustomed to describing everything for the blind man's benefit. 'Keeping a boat here in summer – that'd be fun.' The compartments were

4

hushed. Even the inveterate card-players – the voyage across the Atlantic had taken eleven days – had finally given up.

Apart from the footsteps of an occasional passer-by in the corridor, nothing could be heard but the sound of the speeding train. Dark shapes loomed up on the right: mountains.

'Just think,' said Kuert, 'you'll be home by tonight.'

'With luck.' Josef Kürzinger came from Radolfzell, a small German town near the Swiss border. He had been a schoolmaster there before the war. Wounded by a shell splinter during the North African campaign, he'd miraculously survived and been taken prisoner, but he would never see again. 'Sure you won't come with me?'

'I've got to get this business settled first,' Kuert said. 'Then I'll come, that's a promise. Maybe we can get hold of a boat. I'll teach you to sail.'

There was little the two men didn't know about each other. They had occupied adjoining beds in the hospital ward at Philadelphia. Kuert felt for the haversack slung around his neck, his only piece of luggage. His hands were badly scarred. He leant forward as though the other man could see him. 'First I've got to find out exactly what happened. I want to know who sank us.'

'You'll talk yourself into a whole heap of trouble,' said the blind man.

'It's up to me. I'm the only one left – the only one out of three hundred and sixty-five!'

'Asking awkward questions won't bring them back to life.'

'I promised! I promised myself and the others! I've got to speak for them. No one else can.'

The shadows lengthened, gradually immersing the compartment in gloom. All that broke the silence was the monotonous clank and rattle of the wheels.

'At least give me the diary,' the blind man said eventually. 'It'll be safe with me.'

They had written it together. Kuert had told Josef his story in the hospital, and the schoolmaster had advised him to put it down on paper, all of it from first to last.

5

'Be sensible, Fritz. They'll put the fear of God into you.'

'I don't scare that easy.' Kuert couldn't imagine ever being scared again, not after what he'd been through. Death had acquired a different meaning now that he'd looked it in the face. Besides, there was the eternal question: Why me? Why was I the only one to survive? He brought out the notebook in its oilskin wrapper and weighed it hesitantly in his scarred hands. 'Promise me.'

'I won't let it out of my possession. I'll keep it till you need it.'

Kuert put the notebook in the blind man's suitcase and returned to his corner seat. It was now almost dark outside. The ceiling light had come on. They said no more. From time to time a cascade of sparks sped past in the blackness beyond the windowpane.

He dozed fitfully until Josef shook him by the knee, then sat up with a jerk, shivering despite his submariner's greatcoat. 'Don't tell me we're there already?'

'Listen!' A wry smile had appeared on the blind man's face. It hovered around the sockets of the dead eyes, which seemed to lose a little of their fixity.

Kuert could hear voices. More precisely, a tone of voice he'd never thought to hear again. He lowered the window. Constance . . . They were across the frontier – they were back in Germany. Pinpoints of light came bobbing along the darkened platform. He recognized the German MPs by the metal gorgets on their chests. One of them came to an abrupt halt outside the window.

'You, there! Are you crazy? Douse that light!' Kuert pulled the blind down fast. Outside, the raucous voice went on. 'Anyone'd think they'd never heard of the blackout.'

Another voice chimed in. 'High time those lads were brought up to scratch again.'

Kuert silently lifted Josef's suitcase down off the rack. The blind man was still smiling.

'We're home all right,' he said.

★　　★　　★

6

A fortnight later Boatswain Fritz Kuert was escorted to the Admiral's office by two naval ratings.

It was a dismal day. The sleet descending on the barrack square at Buxtehude, headquarters of Naval Operations, turned to grey slush as soon as it touched the ground.

Kuert waited outside in the passage while one of the seamen announced him.

'Boatswain Kuert of the *Doggerbank*, sir.'

'Send him in.'

Kuert marched in and saluted.

The Admiral indicated the chair in front of his desk. He took a file from his flag-lieutenant. 'I'll see this man alone,' he said. He had peculiarly bright, pale blue eyes, and his hair was white with a yellowish tinge. The flag-lieutenant and the seaman left the room.

The Admiral leant forward. 'I want us to be absolutely frank with each other,' he said, doing his best to strike a genial, paternal note. 'Nothing we say leaves this room, is that clear?' He opened the file and smoothed the sheets with his palm. 'Unpleasant business, this. I'm anxious to dispose of it as quickly as possible.'

Kuert said nothing. He was gazing at the map on the wall above the Admiral's head, but his thoughts were elsewhere. *The bastards sank us!* he thought. It occurred to him that those were the first words Stachnovski had uttered when he fished him out of the water after they were torpedoed, but he kept the thought to himself. He could feel the heat of the cast-iron stove on his back. His throat was parched, constricted. He transferred his gaze to the rows of medal ribbons on the Admiral's chest. He had an urge to shout, to bawl out everything he'd meant to say, but he couldn't get his tongue to work. 'It's because of my shipmates, sir, that's all.' That was as much as his anger and agitation would allow him to him say.

'How old are you, Kuert?'

'Twenty-six, sir.'

'Old enough not to go around telling wild tales and asking foolish questions. You're a serviceman, after all.'

'I've never been a serviceman.'

'What do you mean?'

'I'm a merchant seaman, sir. The merchant marine may be on attachment to the navy, but we're an outfit of our own.'

The Admiral shook his head. For the first time, his voice became tinged with annoyance. 'We're all servicemen these days.' He picked up his glasses but didn't put them on as he leafed through the file on his desk. 'We investigated this matter thoroughly.' He looked up. 'At first we couldn't account for the *Doggerbank*'s disappearance. Then came word that a survivor had been picked up. It wasn't until that Spanish tanker fished you out and took you to Aruba that we knew for sure she'd been sunk.'

Kuert sat there stiffly, expectantly. He was becoming less and less mindful of his surroundings. He had ceased to be an insignificant boatswain in the merchant marine, just as the man facing him had ceased to be an all-powerful admiral. He was more than ever conscious of the unseen presence of his shipmates, especially those who had been in the dinghy with him. He felt himself to be their representative, their spokesman – a sole surviving witness on behalf of Paul Schneidewind, the skipper, of Papa Boywitt, the Baltic trawlerman, of Polack Stachnovski, who took such pride in his riding boots, of Jan Bahrend, the spurned sea-cook and renowned yarn-spinner, of Waldemar, the ship's boy, only sixteen and infatuated with a Japanese whore, of—

'We checked the date,' he heard the Admiral say. 'Only one of our submarines reported a sinking on 3 March 1943, and that was *U43*. We summoned the captain to Berlin. After questioning him, we were forced to conclude that. . .' He broke off. 'What's the matter?'

'So it's true!' Kuert gripped the edge of the desk. 'It *was* one of ours! Who was the captain? Who did for us? What's his name?'

The Admiral had turned pale. 'I assumed you already knew,' he said sharply, 'from the way you've been spreading the word.'

'We had our suspicions, but we weren't sure, any of us.' Rage and despair at the others' death had loosened Kuert's tongue. 'He left us to drown – didn't stop to rescue a single one of us! Who was the swine? Who pumped three torpedoes into us and then made himself scarce?'

'Pull yourself together, man!' The Admiral's face had stiffened. 'Who the devil do you think you are, sounding off like this? The case is closed. Our inquiry absolved the U-boat commander of all blame. He acted under a misapprehension, a regrettable but unavoidable misapprehension. If you'll take my advice. . .'

As he listened to the Admiral, it occurred to Kuert that they were talking at cross purposes. Three hundred and sixty-four men had died a miserable death. Some had been drowned or burned alive, others had abandoned all hope of rescue and killed themselves. *A misapprehension.* Was that all? An official report, a few sheets of paper, a figure: 364, one more item in a mass of statistics? And he was expected to keep his mouth shut?

The words came out without his realizing it or grasping the enormity of the situation: an insignificant boatswain in the merchant marine was crossing swords with an admiral in Naval Operations. 'So that's what wiped out the crew of the *Doggerbank*, a misapprehension! Stop hedging and tell me his name!'

The Admiral straightened up with a jerk. 'That's enough!' he snapped. He gestured vaguely at the wall map behind him. 'God Almighty, man! The fate of our country is hanging in the balance, and you have the effrontery to put your personal concerns first!'

He talked on. It was a lengthy peroration – one that seemed directed less at Kuert than at an invisible audience hundreds strong. At last he sat back, his face drained of expression, and closed the file with a snap. 'I had hoped we could settle this matter between the two of us. I can understand your speaking out on behalf of your shipmates, but. . .' He pressed a buzzer. 'I'm sorry, Kuert, you've only yourself to blame. . .'

9

Half an hour later he was escorted back across the barrack square, not by naval ratings this time but by two men in the grey-green uniform of the *Sicherheitsdienst*, the Security Service of Himmler's SS. The snow was falling more heavily, but it still hadn't settled. A couple of sailors paused to watch Kuert go by. 'Been a naughty boy, shipmate?' one of them called.

He didn't feel like talking. His interview with the Admiral seemed unreal, as if it had never taken place. It didn't matter, anyway. His neck was at stake now, and the realization had galvanized him. At least he'd learned one thing, the number of the submarine: *U43*. It wouldn't be hard to discover the captain's name.

They escorted him into an austere, sparsely furnished office. The man behind the desk said nothing, just pointed to the chair facing him. The collar of his uniform tunic was open, and there was a holstered automatic on the belt draped over the back of his chair. In addition to the 'SD' badge on his left sleeve, he wore shoulder straps adorned with two pips.

Kuert didn't know what grade the pips denoted – not a very senior one, but the man's rank was unimportant. His smooth, bland face and inscrutable expression, neither hostile nor friendly, were sufficient identification. He simply sat there, regarding Kuert with almost clinical interest. In front of him lay the file that had previously been on the Admiral's desk.

A typewriter could be heard in the room next door. Someone was pecking away with two fingers, from the sound of it. The man behind the desk got up and went over to the door.

'How's it going?'

'Nearly finished.'

'Bring it in as soon as it's ready for signature. He's here.' The SD man returned to his desk and stood looking down at Kuert. 'I've read the report. Twenty-six days adrift in the Atlantic without food or water. You must have been tough to survive.' His voice was like his face, bland and unemotional. 'I've got a soft spot for tough youngsters.'

'It was a dinghy. No mast, no sail, nothing.'

'I see. When did the Americans first interrogate you?'

'At Aruba.'

'Not later?'

'Later as well.'

'How much did you tell them?'

'There wasn't much to tell.'

'Enough for the BBC to report that the *Doggerbank* had been sunk by a German submarine.'

This was news to Kuert. He flinched as if an unseen chasm had yawned at his feet. Tense and wary now, he said nothing. His instinct for self-preservation was functioning again. It had saved his life more than once.

'Wicked Nazi U-boat captain sends his fellow countrymen to the bottom – a regular sob story. I wonder where the British got it from?' The SD man might have been talking to himself. 'There was only one survivor: you.'

The implication dangled before Kuert like a noose. He had only to put his head in it. 'They must have figured it out for themselves. It can't have been that difficult. Maybe they picked up some radio messages. They couldn't have got it from me, anyway.'

'Really? Why not?'

'Because we didn't know the sub was one of ours. I only found out myself half an hour ago. We had our suspicions, but that's all.'

'And you aired those suspicions?'

'No. Who's going to admit his ship took three torpedoes from a friendly submarine? The Yanks didn't treat us too well, but they didn't torture us.'

'Smart as well as tough, eh? The fact remains, the BBC broadcast that report. Supplying the enemy with information capable of being used to the detriment of the Fatherland. That's one interpretation of your conduct. Men have been executed for less.'

The SD man hadn't raised his voice. His slightly parted lips were set in a frigid smile. The typewriter stopped clattering next door; the clerk came in with some typewritten sheets and handed them over. The SD man took them from him with barely a glance and spread them out on the desk. He unscrewed the lid of an ink bottle and pointed to a pen. 'Perhaps you'd like to sign these,' he said. 'Being as smart as you are.'

It wasn't a lengthy document. He, Fritz Kuert, solemnly undertook never to discuss the circumstances of the *Doggerbank*'s sinking. Date, place, and a dotted line for his signature.

The man at the desk behaved as if the whole affair had ceased to concern him. He buttoned his tunic and buckled on his belt.

Kuert took the pen and signed.

'Both copies.' The SD man's tone was devoid of triumph.

Kuert put his name to the second copy. It was only a scrap of paper, after all. If he could survive twenty-six days in an open boat, he could survive this too.

The SD man blotted both signatures.

'Now do I get to go on leave?' Kuert asked.

'We'll be needing you for a little while longer. We've got a few more questions for you.'

'But—'

'Consider yourself under open arrest,' the SD man cut in. 'You're a bit *too* smart for my liking, Kuert, and it's easy enough to sign a piece of paper. Your case has been referred to us, so we want to wrap it up for good.'

A week later he was taken under guard to Jachmann Barracks at Wilhelmshaven. He remained under open arrest but was free to move around inside the barracks themselves.

Here he was subjected to further interrogation by SD personnel. They kept harping on the broadcast from London, and their questions always followed the same pattern. How much had he told the Americans? How could he have known it was a German submarine that sank the *Doggerbank*? With whom had he discussed the matter? It was as if they wanted to impress on him that he was at their mercy if he didn't keep his mouth shut.

Escape was Kuert's sole preoccupation, and after three weeks an unforeseen opportunity presented itself.

The air-raid warning had sounded that night, as it so often

did, but Kuert could not be induced to take refuge in the shelter. Air-raid shelters were for landlubbers. He was every inch a seaman, and experience had taught him that a seaman's chances of survival were worse below deck. The few extra seconds required to reach the open air in an emergency could spell the difference between life and death.

Tonight, having stationed himself in his usual place near the door when the air-raid siren sounded, he was accosted by an unknown petty officer.

'I've been hoping for a word with you. You must have known Werner Gernhöfer. He was with you aboard the *Doggerbank*.'

The petty officer was a man in his forties. His broad, weather-beaten countenance inspired trust, but Kuert said nothing. If the SD were setting a trap, this was just the type they'd let loose on him.

'Werner was a pal of mine,' the petty officer went on. 'We come from the same neck of the woods.'

Kuert still said nothing, thinking hard. According to this morning's news bulletin the Americans had crossed the Rhine at Remagen. A general retreat would soon be under way. The roads would be swarming with military police patrols. Now, if ever, was the time to take the plunge.

'How did you know about the *Doggerbank*?' he asked warily.

'These things get around,' said the petty officer. 'I'm not being nosy, you understand. It's just that – well, Werner's wife and parents are living here in Wilhelmshaven.'

They'd be bound to have some civilian clothes, Kuert reflected. He wouldn't stand a chance in this naval uniform they'd made him wear. If he wore civvies and carried his seaman's paybook, which the SD had omitted to confiscate, he might just get away with it.

'All they received was a brief notification,' the petty officer went on. 'It simply said the ship went down with all hands. I told old man Gernhöfer about you. He'd like to make your acquaintance.'

Kuert's mistrust revived.

'What if *you* bought it?' the petty officer said. 'Wouldn't your parents like to know more than it says in an official notification?'

'You say he was a friend of yours?'

'We were shipmates.'

'Where?'

'In the *Uckermark*.'

The *Uckermark*. That figured. Gernhöfer had definitely sailed in her, but the SD would know that too.

'I'm confined to barracks.'

'So I gather,' said the petty officer, 'but let me worry about that.'

'All right, I'm on.'

'Fine. See you this time tomorrow night.'

His misgivings revived as soon as the man had gone. They remained with him all the following day. He wasn't summoned for interrogation. Left to his own devices, he lay on his mattress fully dressed, listening to the footsteps in the corridor. The petty officer turned up just before eight. Kuert followed him in silence. It was only a hundred yards across the barrack square to the guard-house. His companion nodded to the sentries. Then they were outside.

It was a modest house situated in a side street. Werner Gernhöfer's wife and parents had assembled in the living-room. Spread out on a table were all the photographs of him they possessed and the last letters he'd written them. They proudly showed Kuert a scatter cushion embroidered in coloured silk with the names of all the ships their Werner had ever sailed in.

Kuert was prevailed on to tell them about the *Doggerbank*'s last voyage. He described the crossing-the-line ceremony, their arrival in Japan, the time they'd spent in Yokohama while the ship was taking on cargo, the judo lessons, the craze for gold teeth. Almost the entire crew of the *Doggerbank* had acquired gold crowns – as a form of investment. He showed them his own five gold teeth engraved with dragons' heads.

He recounted incidents he'd almost forgotten, embellishing them to avoid having to tell the truth.

The two women sat there, outwardly composed, but their composure was only a thin veneer superimposed on grief and despair. One ill-judged word, and they would both have burst into tears.

At last the petty officer came to his rescue. They must go, he said. They had to get back before the sentries changed.

Gernhöfer's father saw them out. He shut the living-room door behind him. 'How did Werner die?' He stood there, a white-haired man leaning on a stick. 'I'd sooner know the truth.'

Kuert told him, but only in broad outline. He embellished the facts yet again. 'You mean he was with you after the ship went down?'

'Yes, he made it into the dinghy. Werner was one of the first to die. Of thirst and exhaustion. The first to go died easier than the rest.' It wasn't true and he knew it. His thoughts kept returning to the clothes. He had to ask about the clothes.

'I wanted to beg a favour,' he said eventually. 'I need some civvies – a jacket and a pair of trousers. I'll return them to you.'

The old man limped over to a cupboard, leaning on his stick. 'Take whatever you need. You're just about Werner's size. His things should fit you.'

Kuert selected a jacket and a pair of slacks. The old man brought him some wrapping paper and a piece of string. At the front door he said, 'They're not to be trifled with, those people. I hope you make it, my boy.'

His chance to escape came three days later, when Allied bombers launched their heaviest raid on Wilhelmshaven to date. He was at his usual post in the entrance to the barrack block when the sirens signalled their approach. He watched the last few stragglers sprinting across the parade ground to the shelter.

The sirens were still wailing. Searchlights groped their way across the low cloud cover, anti-aircraft guns opened up.

15

The crump of falling bombs, distant at first, drew nearer. Then a stick of five straddled the barracks. The force of the explosions sent Kuert sprawling.

He scrambled to his feet and dashed along the corridor to his barrack room, extracted the civilian clothes from his haversack and put them on. He could feel cold air streaming in through shattered windows imploded by the blast. Broken glass crunched beneath his shoes. He concealed his uniform under the mattress and made his way outside.

The bombs had completely flattened the guard-house beside the gates leading to the main road. A building was on fire nearby, and the flames had tinged the overcast with red. Bombs were still falling, but that was all to the good.

He set off at a run, oblivious of everything save his single-minded determination to get out of the city, out on the open road. His way was barred by some men wearing the blue armbands of air-raid wardens, but he dodged them and ran on, panting hard, through the blazing streets.

At last he paused in a field. The thunder of the anti-aircraft guns had died away, the sky behind him was crimson. Darkness closed in, strangely still and menacing. All he could hear was the distant hum of departing bombers high overhead.

By day he slept in isolated haystacks or woods; at night he trudged on, keeping to the minor roads. His destination was Hamburg.

He often thought of the *Doggerbank* during those days on the run. It may have been hunger, or solitude and the fact that he was as solely dependent on himself as he had been in the dinghy, when his only aid was the will to survive.

He reached Hamburg on the morning of the fifth day, avoided the Elbe bridge and crossed the river by Ferry No. 7. He was now on familiar territory, having often signed on at Hamburg in the past. He waited for nightfall before making his way to the house in Sierich Strasse.

He was in luck. Harry Purrmann, a seaman like himself and thoroughly trustworthy, was at home. They'd sailed together many times. They'd even been shipwrecked together when the *Savona*, a German freighter, was torpedoed by a British submarine.

But Purrmann couldn't hide him. His ship was sailing in the morning, and the landlord was an enthusiastic Nazi, a snooper. Purrmann went off in search of somewhere Kuert could lie low.

He was back within a couple of hours. 'I've got just the man, a ship's engineer, but he'd like to take a look at you before he decides.'

A fourth-floor flat in Jungfrauenthal, a Hamburg suburb. Hugo Schulz, ship's engineer, looked Kuerz over and asked a few questions. Then he nodded: the fugitive was welcome to stay.

They fixed him up a bed in the roof space. There were air raids almost nightly, but he had to remain there. He couldn't afford to show his face or leave his hiding-place, not ever.

Sometimes his meals were brought him by the girl who later became his wife. Sometimes, though only for a few minutes, Schulz himself came bearing the latest news of the Allied advance.

Kuert spent the rest of the time alone, alone day and night with his memories of the *Doggerbank*, 'my ship,' as Stachnovski always called her.

He would often awake in the small hours, haunted by horrific visions. And, as he lay there in the darkness, his shipmates would come alive once more.

PART ONE

THE SHIP

He had never forgotten the morning he first saw the *Doggerbank* in mid Atlantic. And what a strange ship she was, a regular water-gypsy.

The date was 23 June, 1942, the place a rendezvous code-named 'Nelke' [Carnation]. It was there, south-west of the Cape Verde Islands at 13° north, 26° west, that the *Charlotte Schliemann*, a tanker laden to the gunwales with fuel oil, spare parts and provisions, had been replenishing some U-boats and the auxiliary cruiser *Michel*, alias Ship 28. This spot off the west coast of Africa was often employed as a rendezvous by 'milch cows', as tankers like the *Charlotte Schliemann* were known, and by ocean-going U-boats on patrol.

Boatswain Fritz Kuert could still remember every detail of that fine, windless morning: the pots of mouse-grey paint with which they were daubing the *Charlotte Schliemann*'s wireless office, the dark blue sea with its long Atlantic swell, and the moment when the ship emerged from the haze that veiled the horizon like a gauze curtain.

Off-watch members of the tanker's crew lined the rail as the vessel slowly approached. Kuert had stopped work and joined the two forecastle lookouts, who were observing the new arrival through binoculars.

'Jesus,' said one of them, 'what a shabby old tub!' Kuert would have asked to borrow his glasses, but he still felt like an outsider aboard the *Charlotte Schliemann* and had few friends among the crew. The tanker had inspired him with instant dislike.

The 'shabby old tub' drew steadily nearer. Kuert would have guessed her to be a Britisher from her silhouette, which displayed a typically flush deck-line running from stem to stern. The bow bore no name that he could see, nor was there any port of registry visible on the stern. The odd-looking vessel's approach hadn't signalled a call to action stations, however, so he concluded that the *Charlotte Schliemann*'s skipper must be expecting her.

'You can say that again,' the other lookout chimed in. 'A real floating slum.'

The approaching vessel had clearly been a long time at sea. They'd given her a lick of grey paint at some stage, but the original paintwork was showing through: black on the hull, canary yellow on the upperworks.

She went astern and stopped, riding the long swell barely a cable's length away. Kuert saw a signalman on the wing of the nameless vessel's bridge flash a message, heard an engine start up. Moments later a launch rounded the black-and-grey bow and ploughed a curving furrow of foam through the dark blue water.

Kuert was standing near the accommodation ladder when the launch made fast to the side of the *Charlotte Schliemann*. As soon as the officer from the strange ship came aboard he hailed the young seaman who had remained in the launch.

'Hey, what ship are you?'

'Us?' The youngster glanced back over his shoulder. 'We're the *Doggerbank*.'

Kuert was a good judge of his fellow seamen. From the way this one had looked at his ship and the way his eyes lit up, he could tell she was a good ship despite her shabby exterior.

The crewmen off watch continued to make derisive remarks.

'Foreign-built?' Kuert asked.

'British,' the young seaman replied. 'The auxiliary cruiser *Atlantis* captured her in the Indian Ocean a year ago. Used to be the *Speybank*. Now she's the *Doggerbank* – or the *Stewbank*, *Leveybank*, or *Inverbank*, depending on circumstances.'

The youngster was wearing white ducks and an open-necked white shirt, the hot-weather uniform of the merchant marine. His thin, pale face had never seen a razor. A ship's boy probably, sixteen at most.

'Any more of you from the merchant marine?' Kuert asked.

'The whole crew.'

'Been with her long?'

'This is my first trip.'

'Who owns her?'

'Hansa.'

Kuert stared fixedly at the ship as she rode the swell. He

absorbed her every detail: the bridge superstructure, the two masts, the derricks, the lifeboats, the gun in the stern, the men leaning on the rail.

'Who's your skipper?'

'Our captain? Schneidewind.'

'Paul Schneidewind? Of the *Tannenfels*?'

'Could be. Nearly all our lot are former Fels-folk.'

The *Tannenfels*, *Geierfels*, *Freienfels* and *Reichenfels* were all Hansa ships, hence the nickname 'Fels-folk'. They were also ships in which Kuert had sailed in the past. He continued to gaze at the *Doggerbank*, spellbound by the sight of her. He now saw — or so it seemed to him she seemed — beautiful beyond compare.

'Your name?' [...]

Kuert [...] at him curiously.

'What about the cargo mate?'

'His name's Johnny Jahr.'

'And the [...]'

'[...] I can't remember. His real name is—'

'You don't tell me. Ian Behrendt! The best-loved, most-hated [...] Still got a thing about sauerkraut, eh?' [...] an answer. 'That only leaves Papa Boywitt and Fritz [...] great big fellow with a mouthful of baby teeth.'

'They're all on board.'

'The whole bunch? You don't say!' The floating slum had metamorphosed itself into the finest vessel Kuert had ever set eyes on. 'Are you the ship's boy?'

The youngster nodded. 'My name's Waldemar Ring.'

'Right, Waldemar: as soon as you get back, have a word with one of them, preferably Karl Gaides or Johnny Jahr. This is a lousy ship, tell them. Tell them it's the lousiest berth I've ever had. No laughs, no kindred spirits. I'm eating my heart out here. They've got to get me off this tub. I want out, understand?'

'I'll try.'

'And don't forget to tell them I don't give a damn what I do on board. I'll scrape all the rust off your old tin can. I'll repaint her from bridge to waterline. I'll even help Jan in the galley if I have to, just as long as they get me out of here.'

'What name shall I say?'

'Tell them "For Fatherland and *lire*." That had been their slogan in the days when they were paid in Italian currency for ferrying troops and equipment from Italy to the North African front in the *Freienfels* and the *Geierfels*, two cargo ships of which both had been sunk on the same day by a Greek submarine.

'For Fatherland and *lire*?'

'Yes, lad, and I'm Signor *Lire* in person.'

Those men across the water were his old bunch, his old outfit, an outfit without a flag: men of the merchant marine, seamen, civilians whom the war had condemned to die like members of the armed forces.

An hour later Johnny Jahr came over in the launch; three hours later the *Charlotte Schliemann*'s second mate sent for him and announced that Captain Schneidewind urgently needed a boatswain and had asked the skipper to let him go. 'They seem to think pretty highly of you,' the second mate added rather sourly.

Kuert stifled a retort, just waited for his papers. He was already at the door when the second mate said, 'Well, let's hope the change brings you luck. They have an odd name for that tub. Ask them when you get there.'

He packed his things. The most important item was a homemade survival kit. It always lay ready to hand at the foot of his bunk, a broad belt of stiff sailcloth with a clasp-knife and canteen attached, the latter permanently filled with rum. He had devised and made it himself after yet another of his ships, the *Savona*, was sunk in the Mediterranean and he spent two days in the water before being picked up. His shipmates in the *Charlotte Schliemann* scoffed at it, but that didn't worry him. He donned the belt every night before turning in and wore it whenever things got hairy. He also owned a special pair of shoes which he kept in a shoe-box. A cobbler in Sorrento had made them to his specifications: tight-fitting, thin soles, Russia leather. You could swim in them and hardly know you were wearing them.

Kuert buckled on his survival belt, picked up his suitcase and shoe-box and headed for the accommodation ladder.

He stood with his legs braced apart as the launch cut through the long swell, ducking to avoid occasional showers of spray. He didn't once look back. All his attention was centred on the *Doggerbank*.

They threw a line and a Jacob's ladder over the rail. He was half-way up the ladder before the boat had even made fast.

They had all turned out to welcome him: Karl Gaides, the *Doggerbank*'s mate, wearing shorts and stripped to the waist, a walking museum of the tattooist's art; 'Polack' Stachnovski, so called because he came from Upper Silesia, reddish-blond but still beardless except for a few sparse hairs between his chin and lower lip; Jan Bahrend, the cook with German and American nationality, elegant as ever in his silk shirt and starched chef's hat; and Karl 'Papa' Boywitt, the silent, self-effacing Baltic trawlerman. The rest were new to him.

Their faces bore a resemblance to the ship. They were grey, the faces of men long at sea, weary and lined with many days and nights of nervous tension.

'Well, sonofabitch,' said Jan Bahrend, 'if it isn't Signor *Lire* himself! Another sauerkraut-eater, all we needed.' He beamed all over his face.

'Fritz!' Stachnovski gripped Kuert by the shoulders, spun him around, scrutinized the survival belt. 'It's our Fritz all right, complete with all the trimmings.' He gave the others a meaningful glance. 'Since when did they let you aboard another ship?' Those who understood the allusion laughed.

Karl Gaides stepped forward and put his hands on his hips. 'Boatswain Kuert,' he said in an assumed voice, 'what are you doing here again?'

It was a perfect imitation of someone familiar to every merchant seaman in the Mediterranean: Commander Koch of the maritime personnel office at Naples. Koch, who was

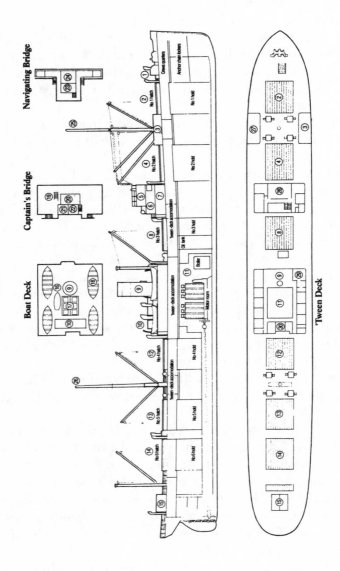

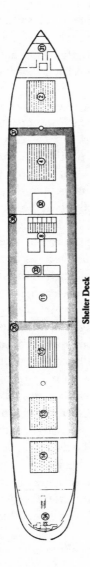

Shelter Deck

1   Weather cowl over stairs to crews quarters
2   No 1 Hatch and hold
3   Side house and galleys
4   No 2 Hatch and hold
5   Wheel and chart-room
6   Captain's accommodation
7   Pantry and dining saloon
8   No 3 Hatch and hold
9   Funnel
10   Engine room
12   No 4 Hatch and hold
13   No 5 Hatch and hold
14   No 6 Hatch and hold
15   Port office and hospital
16   Dinghy
17   Bullseyes housing covering engine room
18   Lifeboats
19   Stairs
20   Captain's dayroom
21   Captain's bedroom
22   Toilet
23   Chartroom
24   Bridge
25   Foremast
26   Aftermast
27   Stores & wc
28   Officers quarters
29   Engineer's accommodation
30   Cook's quarters
31   Crew's quarters
32   Specie room
33   Freshwater tanks
34   Steering gear
35   Twin tier bunks for 75 men
36   Twin tier bunks for 28 men
37   Bunks for 120 men

responsible for crew allocation, had eventually assigned Kuert to shore duties because he had been sunk four times in the space of a year. Four of the ships in which he'd sailed had been torpedoed by enemy submarines or bombed to destruction by enemy aircraft. His former shipmates had actually witnessed the scene in the personnel office which Gaides was now re-enacting.

Gaides threw up his hands. 'I'm not letting you set foot in another ship, Boatswain Kuert! Out of my sight, I never want to see you here again! Every ship I assign you to goes down.'

'No more ships for you, Boatswain Kuert!' Stachnovski yelled. Then they all crowded round, shook his hand, bombarded him with questions. Standing there in their midst, with their friendly laughter ringing in his ears, he felt at home once more.

Later he discovered what the *Charlotte Schliemann*'s second officer had meant. The crew of the *Doggerbank*, alias Ship 53, an auxiliary cruiser of 5154 tons, had an odd English nickname for her: 'the never-come-back liner'. They uttered it with a certain pride. It was a kind of talisman, an insurance against disaster. They never for one moment imagined that disaster might actually strike. In their eyes the *Doggerbank* had become a legend, a lucky ship capable of the most foolhardy exploits and commanded by a skipper who was a credit to his profession: Paul Schneidewind, a man seemingly without nerves, forever spick and span in his merchant marine tunic with the captain's four rings. Anyone would have thought it was still peacetime and he standing on the bridge of one of the fast Hansa Line freighters that plied between Bremen and the East Indies.

On 27 June, 1942, four days after Boatswain Fritz Kuert had transferred from the *Charlotte Schliemann* to the *Doggerbank*, Captain Schneidewind received a signal ordering him to Japan.

In August the *Doggerbank* reached Yokohama and underwent a refit. She left the Japanese port on 17 December, having been converted into a blockade-runner, one of the lightly-armed vessels that sneaked past Allied naval patrols carrying cargoes essential to the German war effort, mainly raw materials. Thereafter she put in at Kobe on 19 December, Saigon on 30 December, Singapore on 7 January, 1943, and Batavia on 10 January. At all these ports the *Doggerbank* took on valuable items of freight: fats, oils, precious metals, crude rubber. Then, fully laden, she set off on the long and perilous voyage home. Her destination was the port of Bordeaux, over 10,000 miles away.

The *Doggerbank* rounded the Cape of Good Hope and successfully negotiated the Atlantic 'narrows' between West Africa and Brazil, an exceptionally hazardous sea area patrolled by Allied aircraft.

At the end of January the ship was overflown by an American Liberator. The crew spread a Union Jack on deck, and the imposture worked as so often before.

On 23 February, 1943, the *Doggerbank* entered the vicinity of a large task force of Allied warships. Their radio messages filled the ether for days on end, but the blockade-runner was in luck once more. Fate had reserved her for an end even more cruel than destruction at the hands of the enemy.

By the third day of March, 1943, the *Doggerbank* was nearing the Azores. Thanks to fine weather and favourable currents, she had made better time than on the outward voyage. Not a masthead, not an aircraft was in sight. The sparkling, dark blue sea revealed no sign of life.

The watches had changed at noon. The lookouts silently manned their posts.

At 12.10 Seaman Richard Binder looked down from his perch in the foremast crow's nest, sixty feet above the deck.

'Nothing in sight!'

His voice carried the length of the ship. Those on deck who heard it froze for a moment, then went on with what they were doing.

The crow's nest lookout had reported nothing else for the past week, ever since they crossed the equator, but everyone knew that appearances could be deceptive. Here, north of the line, the risk of being detected by enemy aircraft was many times greater than it had been further south.

No one knew that better than the skipper.

Paul Schneidewind had been on the bridge for hours. As he swept the horizon yet again with his binoculars, he couldn't banish the thought of what might happen at any time. Another blockade-runner, the *Friedberg*, had followed the same route only a few days before. A hundred and fifty miles north of the Azores the ship had met up with three German submarines under orders to escort her back to France. Four hundred miles west of the Iberian coast the *Friedberg* had been spotted by an Allied reconnaissance plane whose pilot promptly radioed her position to a British cruiser. Not even the three U-boats had been able to prevent her from being shot to pieces and sent to the bottom.

Did Schneidewind know this? Whatever the truth, visions of sinking ships and drowning men preyed on his mind and had left their mark on his face, which was strained and hollow-cheeked with fatigue. He was in his early forties but looked ten years older.

'This weather isn't going to hold.' Langhinrichs, the *Dogger-bank*'s first officer, was standing beside the captain with a signalman and lookouts close at hand.

A few pale, feathery clouds were gathering in the west. Schneidewind lowered his glasses and nodded silently. There was nothing around them but dark blue sea and an immensity of sky, nothing to be heard but the pounding of the engines and the hiss of foam along the hull.

'We're getting pretty near the Azores, sir,' said Langhinrichs. 'How soon do you think we'll pick up our escort?'

They were rapidly approaching the sea area where a German submarine had been instructed to assume protection of the ship and her precious cargo. Like the ill-fated *Friedberg*, the *Doggerbank* was to make for Bordeaux across the Bay of Biscay, an exceptionally dangerous part of the voyage.

'Today or tomorrow, I reckon,' Schneidewind replied.

'The sooner the better,' said Langhinrichs.

Schneidewind looked out over the broad, deserted expanse of sea. Their main aid to survival was unremitting vigilance. The skipper was liked and respected for his imperturbability, his lack of rank-consciousness – he treated the ship's boy with neither more nor less consideration than his first officer – and the way in which he combined tolerance with discipline. A week ago he had imposed a strict ban on alcohol, doubled up the lookouts and posted them throughout the ship. There were four in the foremast and crow's nest alone, his best men. Exempted from all other shipboard duties, they kept two-hour watches instead of four.

'Keep your eyes skinned.' Schneidewind nodded to the lookouts and retired to the chart-house, leaving a faint whiff of eau de cologne in his wake. It was his one weakness, this fondness for French perfumes, and he indulged it almost as if he were trying to compensate for his otherwise austere life-style.

'Helmsman relieved, course zero-three-five,' the helmsman reported. Hans Hencke was a beanpole of a man at least six feet six inches tall.

'Very good.' Although every British ship bound for England from West Africa steered this course, Schneidewind's choice of route was deliberate. The *Doggerbank* not only behaved like a Britisher; she really was one, in a sense, having been built on Clydeside in 1926 and named the *Speybank*. Over the years the yard had turned out seventeen ships of the same class, vessels as alike as peas in a pod, so Schneidewind had a wide variety of genuine names to choose from and could, if need be, change his spots every day. This capacity for disguise was his ship's greatest asset, and one that had many times saved her from destruction.

'What's happened to that goddamned U-boat, sir?' Hencke said. 'Will it show up soon?'

Schneidewind didn't reply. He was watching four men doubling round the deck, arms pumping. He left the bridge and reached the foot of the companionway just as they were starting on another circuit.

'Boywitt,' he called, 'here a minute. What are you up to?'

The other three men were unknown to him. Youngsters of eighteen or so, they belonged to the group of navy personnel assigned to his ship at Yokohama.

Boywitt came over, a forty-year-old whose leathery cheeks bespoke his years as a sea-going fisherman.

'Well, Boywitt, what's all this? You were detailed as a lookout, weren't you?'

The foursome stood there, chests heaving under their open-necked, sweat-sodden shirts.

'Toughening-up course, sir,' Boywitt replied, out of breath. 'Ten times round the ship and twenty knees-bends after each circuit.'

'On whose orders?'

Boywitt hesitated. His broad face creased in a sheepish smile. The other three, who were hovering behind him, remained silent too. Schneidewind could see red burn scars on their exposed flesh.

On 30 November an explosion had devastated the *Uckermark*, a German ship berthed at Yokohama, killing 56 and injuring hundreds of men in the *Uckermark* herself and in two other vessels, the *Nanking* and the *Thor*. The *Doggerbank* had taken all the walking wounded on board before sailing, most of them suffering from minor burns. There were over two hundred of them, so the *Doggerbank*, with a normal complement of 109, was carrying a total of 365 men on this voyage, an additional burden of responsibility for Schneidewind to bear.

'Well, who was it?'

'Lieutenant Fischer,' Boywitt said reluctantly.

Fischer, a naval lieutenant from the *Thor*, had also joined them at Yokohama. He had soon earned a reputation as a martinet who considered the crew of the *Doggerbank* a bunch of indisciplined civilians and proposed to spruce them up in his own fashion.

'Why?'

Boywitt looked down at himself. 'Shirt hanging out, sir.'

'What about you three?'

The naval ratings glanced at each other but said nothing.

'The same,' said Boywitt.

'All right, that's enough,' Schneidewind said. 'How many circuits have you done?'

'This was the last, worse luck,' said Boywitt, still breathing heavily.

Afterwards, back on the bridge, Schneidewind turned to his messenger. 'Lieutenant Fischer to the bridge,' he said, and raised his binoculars again.

The crow's nest lookout, who had orders to report every ten minutes, sang out his ritual 'Nothing in sight!'

It was 12.15 p.m., fifteen minutes before the submarine surfaced.

The story of the toughening-up course and its premature conclusion was all round the ship within minutes, but most of the *Doggerbank*'s crew were old sea-dogs and, as such, fatalists. Fischer had thrown his weight about from the first, so they showed their faces on deck as seldom as possible. They little suspected how many of them would lose their lives as a result.

Boywitt had gone aft to his quarters above the tiller flat, which he shared with Karl Gaides, Stachnovski, Jan Bahrend and Kuert.

'Have you eaten yet?' Kuert asked him.

At twenty-five, he was the youngest of them.

Boywitt shook his head. 'Not hungry.' He stretched out with his arms behind his head and stared into space. They didn't call him 'Papa' for nothing. Older than all of them except Bahrend, he was a quiet, taciturn man who kept himself to himself. He said his prayers night and morning, kneeling beside his bunk as if he were quite alone, but no one would ever have dared to josh him about it.

'I'll bring you some,' Kuert said.

It was the usual Saturday midday meal, smoked ham with sauerkraut and fried potatoes. When Kuert returned with two helpings, Stachnovski rolled over on his bunk and stuck his hand out.

'I'll have that.'

Kuert cocked an eyebrow at Boywitt, who nodded.

'He's welcome to it.'

Having wolfed the lot, Stachnovski put the tin plate on the floor beside two others. He was permanently hungry, however much he ate, but he never gained a pound.

'Sonofabitch, how I hate sauerkraut!' Jan Bahrend thrust the plates aside in disgust with his foot. '*Verdammte Krautfresser*, goddamned cabbage-eaters, that's what you are!'

Other German seamen tended to garnish their native tongue with snippets of English, whereas Bahrend spoke English garnished with snippets of German. He'd spent thirty years of his life in America, serving in the US Army during the First World War and acquiring US citizenship. Not far off sixty by the time the Second World War broke out, not that he ever admitted to his age, he'd made an impulsive and adventurous return to his native land.

'You'd eat sauerkraut if it was your last meal on earth,' he began again.

Boywitt's face stiffened. 'Don't talk like that,' he said in his earnest way.

'You would, I tell you, and you probably will, on this goddamned tub. It's all my replacement knows how to dish up.' Bahrend re-tied his white sweatband, the only remaining token of his former status as the *Doggerbank*'s cook.

'At it again?' Gaides growled. 'Can't you talk about something else?' He was lying on his bunk stripped to the waist. His appendectomy scar was still bandaged. He had undergone surgery in Japan, and the wound had broken open again.

Jan Bahrend's stint as the ship's cook had been terminated at Yokohama. It wasn't that he couldn't cook. He'd owned a modest restaurant in New York. Gaides had eaten there and could testify to the quality of its cuisine. The trouble was that Bahrend couldn't make do with anything less than a superabundance of all ingredients, so the meagre, carefully computed rations aboard a ship like the *Doggerbank* had defeated him from the start. He'd gone at them like a bull at a gate and produced the most sumptuous meals, but only for a week or two. After that the crew were on short commons: Bahrend had used up the bulk of his stores.

Replaced as cook by Schneidewind because of mutinous mutterings among the men, Bahrend was now an ordinary seaman. Even though the skipper let him continue to draw cook's pay, demotion was a blow that had badly wounded his self-esteem.

'Know something?' he said. 'When we get to Bordeaux I'm going to cook you a meal fit for a king. *Dreizehn Gänge*, thirteen courses, that's a promise!'

'Thirteen courses!' groaned Stachnovski. 'Holy Mary, how long it seems since we went through thirteen courses!' He clutched his mop of unruly red hair. 'Remember that time back in Yokohama. . .'

For a while they wallowed in memories: the rickshaw rides, the fat cigars they used to smoke, the white tie and tails they'd all hired at Bahrend's insistence, the New Grand Hotel, the thirteen-course dinner and the morning after, when all they had left was a one-sen piece, just enough to put in the brothel's pinball machine, which won you a whisky toddy if you notched up 6,000 points.

'In Bordeaux I'll start us off with. . .'

'For God's sake stop talking about food!' said Stachnovski.

He had gone over to Gaides's bunk. He was wearing a pair of Russia leather riding boots acquired in Japan and a huntsman's green jacket over his bare chest, on which a tattooed representation of the *Doggerbank* was faintly visible.

'Fritz did a rotten job on me,' he said. 'It didn't last. Three weeks, and there's almost nothing left.' He gazed admiringly at the tattoos on Gaides's torso, which looked like the illustrations in a tattooist's catalogue. A massive ocean liner steamed diagonally across the mate's chest. His back displayed a crucifix and, in the background, the misty face of a girl in nurse's uniform. His left arm was encircled by a snake, his right bore a 'seaman's grave'.

'The fellow who did those,' said Stachnovski, 'was a real

artist.' He continued to gaze, spellbound. The little, rodent-like teeth that used to be his most distinctive feature had gone. His mouth was an Aladdin's cave of gold crowns, the front ones engraved with dragons' and lions' heads.

Gaides had set the fashion in this respect too. He'd had his sound teeth filed down and capped with gold as a hedge against hard times.

'Fritz bungled it,' Stachnovski pursued. 'He couldn't even do my ship properly.' He always referred to the *Doggerbank* as 'my ship'.

'I'll get you some decent soot next time,' Gaides told him. 'You used the wrong kind.'

For want of suitable ink, Kuert had tattooed Stachnovski's chest with engine-room soot. It looked quite good at first, but it had soon begun to fade.

'You must have another go at it before Bordeaux,' said Stachnovski.

'Bordeaux?' Bahrend said. 'I wouldn't be so goddamned sure you'll see it again. Did any of you catch sight of Fujiyama when we sailed?'

Nobody spoke. They looked at him as he sat there filling his pipe, a tall, cadaverous figure with bushy grey eyebrows and pendulous cheeks.

No one knew how seriously to take Jan Bahrend when he embarked on one of his flights of fancy. His reputation as a spinner of yarns was legendary, and most of them were grim, sinister tales, all of which ended with their ship being sunk by shell-fire or torpedoes. On deck he would buttonhole young, inexperienced seamen, draw them to the rail, and point to some imaginary spot in the distance. '*Siehst du ihn?*' he would say. 'He's down there waiting for us!'

His stories were popular nonetheless, especially the ones about his years in America. People would listen to him holding forth for hours on end, always with such an earnest, melancholy expression that they could never be certain whether or not he was pulling their leg. But that didn't matter. The younger seamen enjoyed his yarns and were quite prepared to sacrifice a cigar for half an hour's worth, with the result that most of the cigars in circulation ended up in Jan Bahrend's locker.

'You know what the Japs say,' he went on. ' "He that sees the Sacred Mountain when he sails will come safe home." I didn't see it. Did *you*?'

They all preserved an uneasy silence. Already hot and stuffy, the air in their quarters seemed suddenly more so.

'You and your blather,' Gaides said irritably. 'It's getting me down.'

'I couldn't see Fujiyama when we sailed,' Bahrend persisted. 'Not a sign of it, just cloud. Could you?'

The monotonous rhythm of the engines slowed.

'Sonofabitch,' said Bahrend. 'This lousy war!'

Abruptly the cramped compartment was filled with the sound of the ship's claxon sounding action stations.

Kuert buckled on his survival belt as he ran. The klaxon was still blaring when he reached the deck.

He could see Captain Schneidewind and his officers standing on the bridge with their glasses levelled. He himself could detect nothing on the mirrorlike surface of the sea.

When the klaxon died away he heard the crow's nest lookout call, 'Still at green one–zero, sir. Hard to make out at this range. Small vessel, no smoke.' The *Doggerbank* was gliding along now, only just under way. Nothing could yet be seen from the bridge. Schneidewind turned to his third officer. 'Take a look, Heuer.' Heuer was acknowledged to have the keenest pair of eyes on board. The men on the bridge watched him scale the mast and gain the crow's nest. From there he climbed to the truck of the mast, which increased his range of vision by several hundred yards.

Everyone waited tensely. The *Doggerbank* continued to glide across the glassy swell. Then came Heuer's voice from above, hoarse with excitement. 'Could be a submarine, sir!'

It was still impossible to make out anything from the bridge apparently, and Kuert could see nothing but glittering water.

'Not under way,' Heuer reported. 'Stopped, I think. Hard to tell for sure, but it looks like a submarine.'

Langhinrichs glanced at Schneidewind. 'What do you think, sir? Could it be *our* boat?'

Schneidewind took a quick look round. He was pleased and reassured by what he saw because it showed how reliable and well-trained his crew were. Gernhöfer had cleared his gun for action in the stern, and the pair of quadruple 20 mm. cannon flanking the bridge were fully manned.

He gave his messenger some steering orders for the helmsman, and they headed for the unidentified vessel in a wide arc that would put the *Doggerbank* down-sun of it. As they drew nearer, even the men on the bridge could see that it was a submarine.

'They must be fast asleep,' said Langhinrichs. He glanced back at the stern, where the 105 mm. gun was now trained on the stationary vessel. 'We could blow them out of the water.'

Lieutenant Fischer, who had joined them on the bridge, said, 'That's a German boat, no doubt about it. I know the class.'

Still no sign of life aboard the submarine. It lay there, glinting in the sunlight, like a ghost ship.

'Make the recognition signal,' Schneidewind said eventually.

The German war ensign was run up the mainmast and an anchor ball displayed in the bow. A manila rope with eight red firehoses suspended from it was strung between the mainmast and the wireless office.

'Think they've got the message, Captain?' Langhinrichs looked back into the sun, which was high in the sky. 'Surely they must have spotted us by now?'

Schneidewind turned to the signalman. 'Aldis, please.'

The man hurried back with it. Schneidewind could sense them all watching as he climbed to the monkey island atop the chart house. The old Morse signalling lamp was part of the *Doggerbank*'s legend. Schneidewind had used it to bluff his way past a British cruiser when ordered to heave to and identify himself.

WHAT SHIP? the cruiser had signalled.

BRITISH INVERBANK FROM NY BOUND DURBAN.

He had played the same trick, time and again, on neutral freighters, British warships, even low-flying enemy reconnaissance aircraft. Once, having inadvertently found himself at dawn in the middle of an Allied convoy, he had spent the entire day in the guise of a Britisher. On another occasion, using the same cover, he had pulled off a considerable feat of seamanship by taking his ship into the heavily guarded roads of Cape Town and laying enough mines to render that important Allied naval base unsafe for several months.

Almost lovingly, Schneidewind raised the lamp and signalled: WHAT IS WRONG?

DO YOU HAVE ENGINE TROUBLE?

CAN WE ASSIST?

No reply.

Schneidewind could still sense the others' eyes upon him. The fact that his men trusted him so implicitly only heightened his sense of responsibility. Only four lifeboats and four liferafts between three hundred and sixty-five men! He considered the matter soberly, without panic, but could not suppress an uncharacteristic pang of fear. Whatever his decision, it was his alone to make. He couldn't check by radio with ISKL [Naval Operations I], the section responsible for his ship: the British and Americans had D/F stations all along the African coast and were able to plot a ship's position in minutes and with deadly accuracy.

Schneidewind wondered if this would prove to be the voyage on which his proverbial good luck finally ran out.

Back on the bridge he handed the lamp to the signaller and turned to the helmsman.

'Half ahead. Steer zero-three-five.' It was their original course.

Hencke repeated the order. 'Half ahead, sir. Course zero three-five.'

The engine-room telegraph rang and the engines' rhythm changed once more.

Schneidewind returned to the wing of the bridge. It was

now 13.00. Half an hour had elapsed since the submarine was first sighted.

'That was a German boat,' Fischer said. 'I'd take a bet on it.'

Schneidewind looked at him as if trying to recall something. 'By the way,' he said, 'this is a ship, not a parade ground. Kindly stop hassling my men.' It was unlike him to say such a thing.

He turned to Langhinrichs. 'Keep the men at action stations.'

He raised his binoculars. The submarine slowly receded until there was nothing in sight but sea, until the whole incident seemed an illusion.

Three hours later, at 15.55, the lookouts made another sighting. It wasn't the same submarine, but they were never to know that, any more than they knew that the *Doggerbank* had entered a sea area in which a group of seven U-boats was preparing to attack an Allied convoy.

None of the U-boats was expecting the *Doggerbank*. None had been informed of the recognition signal prearranged with Naval Operations. They were lying in wait for prey.

The sea area into which the *Doggerbank* was heading was not a traditional U-boat hunting ground. That was the North Atlantic, whose principal supply routes were used by convoys carrying war material from the United States to Britain and from there to Murmansk by way of the North Cape. At this stage, however, the North Atlantic offered U-boats little in the way of easy pickings; in fact they had ceased to be the hunters and become the hunted. The defensive measures employed by the convoys' naval escorts had steadily improved, the U-boats were becoming obsolete. The 'happy times', as German submariners called them, meaning the era of the great convoy battles and successes, were over. The tables had turned with a vengeance. Until summer, 1942, the ratio of sinkings had been one U-boat to twenty Allied ships. Now, in 1943, it stood at two to one against, and many a U-boat failed to score a single kill.

From October, 1942, onwards, therefore, more and more German submarines had been withdrawn from the approaches to the British Isles. It was hoped that the new, improved U-boats with better weapons systems would soon be operational. Meantime, as a stopgap measure, the focus of U-boat operations was shifted further south. Other U-boats were dispatched to the Mediterranean, where Germany's Afrika Korps was being hard pressed in Tunisia, their task being to halt, or at least disrupt, the flow of Allied supplies and reinforcements.

On 27 February, 1943, the German Admiralty received intelligence of a large Atlantic convoy routed south of the Azores and bound for the USA. On 1 March a group of seven U-boats, the 'Tümmler' Group, was instructed to form a patrol line, or cordon, south west of the Azores. The seven boats stationed themselves at intervals of thirty miles on a north-south axis, thereby covering the 180-mile stretch through which the convoy was likely to pass. This operation had been code-named 'Rochen'.

The U-boat at the southern extremity of the patrol line, *U521*, was in all probability the one sighted on 3 March by the *Doggerbank*.

Meantime, the ship was back on her original course and had steamed past *U106*, *U558* and *U202* without seeing them or being seen herself. It was the fifth boat, *U43*, that first sighted the *Doggerbank*.

A copy of *U43*'s war diary, a form of ship's log which was kept on board and is now preserved in the archives of the British Admiralty, records the time of the sighting as 17.00, broad daylight in other words. This fact has an important bearing on any assessment of subsequent events.

When the U-boat captain, *Oberleutnant zur See* [Lieutenant] Hans-Joachim Schwantke, sighted the *Doggerbank*'s faint plume of smoke through his binoculars, *U43* was some ten miles away. She was the first ship *U43* had sighted for weeks, and Schwantke left his place in the patrol line without a moment's hesitation.

Proceeding on the surface, *U43* made its way towards the plume of smoke.

U43 was a celebrated, almost legendary submarine. Its previous commander had been *Kapitän zur See* [Captain] Wolfgang Lüth, the first naval officer to be awarded Germany's highest military decoration, the oak-leaves with swords and diamonds. During his active service as a submarine commander he had sunk 46 merchantmen totalling over a quarter of a million tons, a destroyer, and an enemy submarine. He had also torpedoed and damaged two battleships.

Hans-Joachim Schwantke, a native of Upper Silesia and 25 years old at this time, had inherited *U43* from Lüth in March, 1942. Thereafter, luck seemed to have deserted the U-boat. In the navy since 1936, Schwantke had first served in the cruiser *Karlsruhe* and had later, in April 1940, transferred to submarines. He spent some time on the administrative staff of C.-in-C. U-boats before undergoing his submarine commander's training with the 24th U-boat Flotilla between January and March, 1942.

U43 had sailed from Lorient on 9 January, 1943. This was Schwantke's second patrol aboard, and it had thus far been as abortive as the first.

Late in January *U43* and several other German submarines were deployed against Convoy UC1. The engagement lasted four days, but the convoy was strongly defended. *U43* had not only been unable to attack; it had sustained minor damage from depth charges. After two whole months at sea, its tally of torpedoes was still intact.

Schwantke needed, indeed craved, a success.

It was understandable enough. Lüth, the celebrated ace, had handed over to Schwantke, who had hitherto failed to sink a single ship, not one in the course of a year's command, and didn't boast a single decoration. His reaction on sighting that plume of smoke was hardly surprising. 'At last!', he must have told himself. 'Let's hope none of the other boats gets there first.'

The ship's masts were now clearly visible from the U-boat's

bridge. Schwantke and his men scanned the horizon for other vessels.

'Seems to be on her own,' said the officer of the watch. Schwantke never took his eyes off the ship, whose sunlit silhouette was still an indistinct blur. 'Let's hope she isn't a tiddler,' he said. It sounded like a prayer.

The lookouts called the bearings down through the hatch. Below, the quartermaster sat over his charts, working out the ship's course. Finally he called up, 'Target's course north-east, no zigzag, speed approximately twelve knots.'

Did Schwantke never stop to wonder what a lone ship was doing in this sea area, let alone steering a straight course? Allied ships usually zigzagged their way across the Atlantic to make it harder for German submarines to attack them.

U43 was now so near that the ship had ceased to be a blur. Her silhouette showed up crisply in Schwantke's binoculars. He recorded his observations.

'Vessel of 7,000 to 10,000 tons. Flush-decked. Foremast between hatches one and two. Bridge amidships, mainmast between hatches four and five.'

The details were passed to the officer of the watch, who had gone below and was consulting Lloyd's Register. Nothing broke the silence on the bridge save the monotonous throb of the diesels and the hiss of the bow-wave.

The man in the hatchway straightened up. 'Officer of the watch reports she could be the *Dunedin Star*, sir. Or a Blue Star Liner. Almost certainly British.'

The ship's name was the least of Schwantke's present concerns. That could wait until he'd sunk her and confirmed it by picking up a survivor.

He passed his engine and steering orders below. The roar of the diesels attained a new pitch, the bow-wave rose higher. *U43* was solving the first part of a lethal equation: it was drawing ahead so as to gain bearing on the target and torpedo her at right angles to her course. This the U-boat could only do on the surface, its speed when submerged being insufficient. Schwantke was attacking by the book.

43

The unknown ship made no attempt to zigzag. Quite un-suspecting, it seemed, she continued to hold her course, almost in the U-boat's wake. Only one threat to Schwantke's inten-tions presented itself: he sighted his immediate neighbour in the patrol line, *U66*, commanded by *Kapitänleutnant* Gerhard Seehausen. The two submarines flashed an exchange of rec-ognition signals, and *U66* turned away. *U43* continued its manoeuvre.

Would Schwantke realize his mistake at the last moment? Would something make him think twice? The ship's course? Her crowded deck? The red fire-hoses suspended aft?

But Schwantke had no reason to suspect that this ship was a German blockade-runner. Sea areas in which such ves-sels were expected were declared no-go areas, which meant that U-boat commanders were debarred from attacking un-escorted ships in those waters. Besides, the naval authorities always allowed, in seaman's parlance, plenty of 'slack'. In other words, a blockade runner's expected position was notified several days in advance for safety's sake.

U43 had received no such notification.

The submarine was ploughing along some two miles broad on the *Doggerbank*'s bow. Dusk was falling, but it was still light enough for the naked eye to discern its wake from the ship's bridge.

'I was right after all,' said Fischer. 'It *is* a German boat.'

Schneidewind could tell from the faces of the men around him that they were waiting for him to make a decision.

'Bearing?'

'Red three-zero, sir, and drawing ahead.'

Any doubts Schneidewind may have entertained about the submarine's nationality had evaporated. It was a U-boat right enough, but why hadn't it acknowledged his original signal? Had the lookouts really not spotted them? For that matter, why didn't the boat identify itself even now?

Schneidewind, who knew nothing of the 'Tümmler' Group's seven U-boats and was just as ignorant of the fact that they expected an Allied convoy in the vicinity, could only conclude that he was dealing with one and the same submarine.

As for the staff officers of ISKL, the section responsible for blockade-runners, they knew about the seven U-boats but were ignorant of the fact that the *Doggerbank* had reached the same sea area eight or nine days earlier than estimated. A signal had been sent to her captain on 14 February, warning him not to cross the equator before 5 March, and it was taken for granted that this order had been received.

Schneidewind was a cautious skipper. The U-boat's behaviour certainly puzzled him. In fact it disturbed him so much that he momentarily debated whether to consult Naval Operations by radio. He even discussed this possibility with his officers, which was unusual in a man accustomed to taking decisions on his own.

They eventually decided against such a course. British D/F stations could fix a ship's position over most of the North Atlantic, so the risk of betraying themselves was too great. Using the radio might endanger the U-boat as well as the ship.

Schneidewind raised his glasses and took another look at the submarine. His almost too soft and regular features were imbued with masculine severity by a heavy tan and the lines of fatigue round his eyes. He was smartly turned out as usual. The peaked cap was snow-white, the blue tunic with the four gold rings unmarred by a single crease, the leather of his brown oxfords mirror-like. And, as ever, he smelt rather overpoweringly of French cologne.

The others were still awaiting his decision. At last he nodded to the first officer. 'You can secure the lifeboats.'

The faces around him relaxed. 'Aye-aye, sir,' said Langhinrichs. 'What about the recognition signals?'

Schneidewind glanced at the eight red hoses suspended from the rope between the wireless room and the aftermast. 'Leave them where they are,' he decreed.

'And the guns?'

'The gun crews can stand down, but keep the lookouts on their toes.' He nodded to the others. 'I'll be in my cabin if I'm needed.'

They watched him go in silence. 'Takes everything a touch too seriously, your skipper,' Fischer said. 'Everything but discipline, that is.'

Langhinrichs didn't deign to reply. He leant over the wing of the bridge and called to the boatswain. 'You can secure the lifeboats, Kuert,' he said. 'We should be all right now we've picked up our escort.' His relief was manifest. 'Away you go, and make sure those boats are well secured. You know how lumpy Biscay can get.' The submarine, *U43*, was still ploughing along. The Doggerbank was right in its wake.

Kuert went below as soon as he had attended to the lifeboats. On his way to the galley he caught snatches of conversation from the overcrowded crew's quarters. There was only one topic: their imminent homecoming.

Seamen being superstitious, this subject had so far been taboo. None of them had ventured to speak of it, but now that the U-boat had appeared they all felt as good as home and dry.

Menus aboard the *Doggerbank* followed a set pattern. Saturday's evening meal always consisted of canned sausage, fried potatoes and pickled gherkins, but no one had much of an appetite tonight. Kuert, who was in a hurry to get back to his friends, polished off his plateful fast. On his way aft he bumped into Waldemar Ring, the ship's boy. Waldemar, who had joined the ship as a fifteen-year-old, looked little older now. He was a scrawny youth with spindly arms, and not much more than five feet tall.

'Hey, Fritz,' he said, 'do you realize? Another week and we'll be in Bordeaux. Just think, only another week!'

'You can hardly wait, eh?'

Waldemar looked down at the grey fox-terrier winding around his legs. He and Leo, the ship's dog, were inseparable.

'I've been meaning to ask you something, Fritz. Do you think she'll write to me?'

Kuert could see, even in the dimly-lit passage, that Waldemar's cheeks were crimson. Everyone on board knew the story of the ship's boy and Hanako. Men cooped up together for weeks on end had few secrets from each other.

Hanako was a Japanese girl, a prostitute in a Yokohama brothel. It was Stachnovski who had persuaded Waldemar to accompany him there, Stachnovski himself having run out of money to spend on whores. That was how Waldemar had met Hanako and fallen in love with her, although, so Stachnovski reported later, all he'd done was sit there gazing at her with mute adoration and holding her hand.

'Sure she'll write to you,' Kuert told him.

'You really think so?'

Kuert eyed the scrawny little youngster with a trace of compassion. 'There could even be a letter from her on board, if she handed it in at the dockyard gates before we sailed. You'll get your letter when we reach Bordeaux, you'll see.' He didn't know why he was lying to the boy. It was unlike him to spare a person's feelings and expose him to disappointment.

'Stachnovski's looking for you,' Waldemar said, blushing even harder.

The ship's doctor was examining Gaides when Kuert entered the compartment above the tiller flat.

'More rest,' he ordained at last. 'No arguments, Gaides. Stay in your bunk, and you'll be fit as a fiddle by the time we get to Bordeaux.'

'Cheerful sod,' the Mate said when the doctor had gone. The edgy note in his voice was at odds with his usual easy-going manner. He sat up and peered through the porthole. The *Doggerbank* was gliding almost silently, so it seemed, into the dusk.

Gaides flopped back on his pillow. 'It's a swine of a feeling, stewing down here on your own when the klaxon goes.' He ran his hand over the bare metal of the ship's hull, which was only inches from his bunk. 'Man, were my guts churning, lying here waiting for the balloon to go up! Screw that surgeon!'

'Nothing'll happen now,' Kuert said, 'not with that U-boat around. The most we've got to fear is a daylight attack from the air.' He unbuckled his home-made survival belt and returned it to its usual place at the foot of his bunk. Taking off his lightweight leather shoes, he put them back in their box. The threat had receded. Besides, his nose for danger had never failed him in the past.

Stachnovski pointed to the faded tattoo on his chest. 'You've got to do me again, Fritz, for Bordeaux.' He indicated Gaides. 'He says you used the wrong kind of soot.'

'I'll mix you some more,' Gaides said. 'It won't fade this time, believe me.'

Kuert laughed. 'Maybe it was your piss that didn't work.'

'What's wrong with my piss?'

No doubt about it, Gaides was really edgy tonight.

Kuert fetched the tattooing needles and the stencil, which depicted the *Doggerbank* in outline. Stachnovski held it up against the light on the deckhead. 'Lovely ship, isn't she?'

'Lousy fucking tub!' Jan Bahrend was standing beside his bunk, fumbling with his life-jacket. 'Give me a hand with this, will you?' In contrast to Kuert, he was in the process of putting it on.

Kuert went over to him. 'Planning to wear it all the way to Bordeaux?' he said knotting the strings.

The ex-cook, who was a head taller, looked down at him mournfully. 'I was the best goddamned cook in New York; isn't that good enough for you? You expect me to be able to swim as well? I don't intend to go down with this stinking tub!'

Stachnovski was still holding the stencil to the light. 'Hey, Jan, lay off my ship!' He looked round at Kuert. 'Could you do me a U-boat as well, Fritz?'

Bahrend perched stiffly on the edge of his bunk, the lifejacket enclosing the upper part of his body like a plaster cast. He sat there with the portentous mien of an ambassador in boiled shirt and white tie.

'Know something?' he said solemnly. 'I don't like the look of that goddamned submarine. I don't like it one bit.'

He stretched out on his back with his knees drawn up. The bunk was too small for his lanky frame. No one spoke for a while. The air was filled with the monotonous, unchanging throb of the engines. Quite suddenly, Bahrend went on, 'We've had some good times together, haven't we? We've made it so far, but for how. much longer? We've been too damned lucky. It's too good to last.'

Silence.

Stachnovski looked down at his riding boots. Something in what Bahrend had said touched a chord in him. He'd always dreamed of owning a pair of fine, soft boots like these. He didn't know his father; the swine had run out on his mother. He was the bailiff of a big estate somewhere, so he'd heard. He, Ludwig 'Polack' Stachnovski, had a long-term ambition: one day he would confront his father in riding boots and a green huntsman's jacket, looking like an estate manager himself.

He'd never really counted on fulfilling that ambition, but he was half-way there. He had the riding boots, he had the huntsman's jacket, and he had friends. And all those things he owed to this ship, *his* ship. He'd knocked around all his life. People had always poked fun at his Silesian accent, hence the nickname 'Polack'. His shipmates did so too, but the difference was, they did so good-naturedly, because they were his friends.

He had a sudden urge to tell them how he felt, but words failed him. All he said was, 'Just stop criticizing my ship, that's all.'

'Let's face it, Polack,' Jan Bahrend said. His naturally bloodless face was even paler than usual. 'They'll call our number one of these days. Our luck's bound to run out sooner or later.'

He sat up. His eyes had lighted on the survival belt lying at the foot of Kuert's bunk. 'Give us a pull at your canteen, Fritz.'

He pointed to it, and Kuert could see that his hands were trembling.

'One swig, that's all.'

'Sure,' said Stachnovski, 'one swig apiece. You'll be able to refill it soon enough.'

Kuert, still looking at Bahrend's trembling hands, shook

his head. To grant the ex-cook's request would be tantamount to tempting fate. He never touched the rum in the canteen, never emptied it until a new rum ration was issued, and there wasn't any rum on board the *Doggerbank*. No, that wasn't strictly true: anyone who volunteered to sew a dead shipmate into his sailcloth shroud was rewarded with a whole bottle.

'Sorry, Jan, it's a rule of mine.' He'd sworn never to touch the canteen prematurely, and the vow was two years old. Thirty-six hours he'd spent in the water after the *Aegina* was sunk, but he'd had his rum. Rum was the finest aid to survival a shipwrecked sailor could have. In an extreme emergency you could even drink it diluted with seawater.

'Sonofabitch,' Bahrend said resignedly, 'this ship is drier than Texas.'

Waldemar Ring appeared with a tin mug of engine-room soot. Gaides, who had sent him for it, sat up painfully in his bunk and examined it. 'Okay, all of you, look the other way. I'll fix the stuff so it holds, Fritz, but tattoo him somewhere else. I value my peace and quiet. If he hollers the way he did the last time. . .'

He broke off. The loudspeaker on the bulkhead had crackled into life.

It was nearly three months since Schneidewind had addressed the crew. They were well trained, and there hadn't been any untoward incidents. Everyone froze as his voice rang out, calm and composed as ever.

'We shall soon be reaching our port of destination. I shall see to it that half the crew go on leave immediately. The rest will take their turn when the others are back.

'The Japanese provisioned us generously at Yokohama, especially with tea and coffee. Members of the crew may draw their share of the balance of those supplies from tomorrow onwards.

'One more thing: we are now being escorted by a friendly submarine, but we must remain alert. I know I can rely on you to do just that. That's all.'

The first to speak was Stachnovski. 'Great! The folks back home haven't tasted tea like that for years!'

'Just one swallow,' said Jan Bahrend. 'The whole of my tea ration for one swallow of rum.'

Kuert shook his head. 'Nothing doing.'

'Come on,' Stachnovski urged him, 'time to do my ship.' He turned to Gaides and relieved him of the mug of soot, now mixed into a paste with urine. 'We'll be in the forecastle if you want us.'

Kuert picked up the stencil and needles and followed him out, leaving his home-made survival belt and lightweight shoes at the foot of his bunk. Nothing could happen now, he felt sure, not on this voyage.

Up on the bridge of *U43*, Hans-Joachim Schwantke turned to the officer of the watch. 'We'll attack from dived, just in case she isn't as unescorted as she seems. Let's go.'

Darkness seemed reluctant to fall, as if in league with the unknown ship astern of them, but they couldn't wait any longer. As part of the 'Tümmler' Group, *U43* had received a signal ordering it to close the convoy. If Schwantke was going to attack at all, he had to do so now. The lone ship was too tempting a target. The convoy might be so heavily defended that he would be unable to get off a single torpedo.

Schwantke waited until the last man had disappeared through the upper hatch. He took a last look at the ship as she steamed through the dusk. He had now been on the bridge for hours, but he felt no fatigue, just a mixture of determination and anxiety. Determination to sink the ship at all costs, anxiety lest there was something suspect about the situation. It might be a trap.

His instructors at Flotilla had repeatedly warned him against decoys, lone ships sailing in sea areas commonly traversed by enemy convoys. Armed with depth charges and the most up-to-date defensive aids, they were commanded by experienced British naval officers.

He recalled the stories that had circulated among his fellow trainees, stories relating to such vessels and the U-boats that had been destroyed by them.

The ship, her dark shape standing out against the paler skyline, acquired a sudden look of menace. Schwantke secured the upper lid. Moments later he heard the waves breaking over the fore-casing.

U43 went to ninety feet and levelled off. Schwantke waited for the hydrophone operator to report.

There was no sound but the gentle hum of the electric motors and an occasional steering order. The U-boat had turned and was slowly manoeuvring into an attacking position.

The hydrophone operator called out a string of bearings. 'Course still zero-three-five,' the Quartermaster reported.

Schwantke's misgivings revived. He found the ship's unruffled behaviour disquieting. 'Periscope depth,' he said.

Tilting his cap back, he peered through the eye-pieces and saw the faint pall of smoke, the masts and funnel. He passed his observations to the second lieutenant, who set the values on the calculator.

The ship's dark silhouette was growing steadily broader as she gained bearing on the now slowly-moving submarine.

'Flood tubes one to three,' Schwantke ordered. As if he felt it necessary to explain why he was so hell-bent on putting three torpedoes into the ship when one would have sealed her fate for a certainty, Schwantke felt it necessary to add an explanation:

'Better make absolutely sure of her.'

Tattooing was well under way in the forecastle. The younger seamen, who had gathered round to watch, were highly amused whenever Stachnovski grimaced with pain and bared his dazzling gold teeth.

'Are you making a decent job of it this time?' He was seated on a stool, stripped to the waist and holding the stencil against his chest while Kuert knelt in front of him. 'Ouch!'

'Keep still!' Kuert dipped his needle in the black paste and continued to puncture Stachnovski's skin through the perforated stencil. 'Pity you don't have a bit more flesh on your ribs. I've never known anyone eat so much and stay so thin. You must have worms.'

'Just do me a nice ship,' Stachnovski said.

'Don't worry,' Kuert told him, 'the girls'll love it.' They were all in high spirits and making preparations for their homecoming. Kordes was sitting on his bunk with a vulcanized fibre suitcase beside him. 'Last three pairs!' he called. 'Only four packets a pair!'

Kordes was doing a brisk trade on board: cigarettes for shoes. He'd been a cobbler in peacetime, and a good one. His shoes – plaited manila soles, canvas uppers – had sold like hot cakes. His suitcase was filled with the red packets of R6 cigarettes he'd already obtained by barter.

Danziger, a bull of a man, had put on a silk kimono. He'd bought twenty of them in Japan and was picturing the immediate future for his own and the others' benefit. 'Twenty kimonos equals twenty nights. Those French mam'selles are crazy about them. Twenty free nights!'

Kuert caught sight of Waldemar Ring in the bulkhead doorway with Leo, the ship's dog, nestling against his legs.

'That reminds me, Polack,' he said to Stachnovski in an undertone, 'keep an eye on young Waldemar. He's dead serious about that Japanese tart.'

'Nice girl, Hanako,' said Stachnovski. 'Took a real fancy to him.'

'Yes, but he's expecting her to write to him. Damn it, Polack, you dragged him off to that whorehouse. It's up to you to look after him.'

Stachnovski reflected yet again what a good ship the *Doggerbank* was. Somebody needed him, somebody wanted him to look after a shipmate. Back home in Silesia they called him *Perunie*, or 'Thug'. He might really have turned into a thug if he hadn't ended up in this ship.

'I'll ask the skipper to send us on leave together. How would that be?' Stachnovski said. 'We come from the same part of the world. He's from Hindenburg, I'm from Beuthen. Don't worry, I'll take care of the lad.' He was surprised to hear himself say such a thing, but that was yet another debt he owed the *Doggerbank*. 'This tub's getting filthy,' he said. 'They caught the fiftieth rat yesterday, so what makes her such a damned good ship to sail in? Can you tell me why?' Abruptly, he dried up.

'Were you at sea before the war?' Kuert asked. They might have been alone together.

'No, I was a country boy. When the war came I thought the grub would be better at sea. How about you? What keeps you in this outfit?'

'With me it's the pay,' Kuert said. 'The folks back home don't have it as good as us. If I've got to risk my neck, I tell myself, I may as well do it for twice the money and see a bit of the world as well. You can put something by for a rainy day, too. Still, when I think how keen I was to see some action. . .'

'The grub's not so hot,' Stachnovski said, 'but from other angles. . . I can't help thinking of them sometimes, butchering each other on the Eastern Front.'

For a moment Kuert remembered the sensation he'd had when coming aboard the *Doggerbank*, the feeling that he was at home. But there was something else. Didn't they, the men of the merchant marine, have the best of it in this war? They were seamen first and foremost. Even the crews of enemy ships were seamen like themselves and subject to the same, overriding law of the sea.

'Hey,' said Stachnovski, 'you're day-dreaming.'

Kuert carefully removed the stencil.

'Finished?' Stachnovski inquired. 'How does it look? Good?'

Kuert nodded.

Stachnovski rose and squinted down at his chest. 'Anyone got a mirror?' he demanded of the forecastle at large.

In *U43*, the fore-ends reported by voice-pipe that tubes one to three were flooded and ready for firing.

'Range one thousand metres.' Schwantke could detect no lights on his target. She had darkened ship but was holding her course.

It was deathly quiet aboard the U-boat. Every member of

the crew knew his job. Silent routine had been ordained and the men were padding around in their stockinged feet.

The hydrophone operator sat hunched over his equipment. The radio had already been tuned to the 600 metres international emergency frequency in case they could pick up the ship's distress signal and learn her name when they surfaced after attacking.

It was 20.55 when the bow-caps over the torpedo tubes swung open. Schwantke clamped his eyes still tighter to the eyepieces, then slowly raised his arm. Everyone waited for his signal.

Kuert was standing beside Stachnovski, who was inspecting the completed tattoo with the aid of a small hand mirror. They were right at the foot of the forecastle ladder, twelve steps down from the main deck.

Waldemar Ring was on his way from the galley to the Captain's cabin with some coffee for Schneidewind. The ship's boy was in high spirits. He had learned from the Petty Officer in charge of mail that the *Doggerbank* was carrying three sealed sacks of letters. With the ship's dog trotting after him, he quickened his steps to ensure that the skipper's coffee didn't go cold before it reached its destination.

Jan Bahrend paused irresolutely in the doorway of the stern cabin. He was due to relieve the helmsman at 21.00. Kuert's survival belt was still at the foot of his bunk. Karl Gaides, lying on his side facing the hull, was engrossed in a tattered paperback.

One quick swallow, thought Bahrend. Gaides wouldn't notice, and even if he did he wouldn't tell. Just one goddamned swallow! Abruptly, he pulled himself together and continued on his way.

Karl Boywitt, the former trawlerman, was bound for his favourite spot, the monkey island. He would spend long hours sitting up there all by himself, gazing at the constellations that looked so different in these latitudes from the way they looked back home. If he gazed at the night sky for long enough it underwent a transformation, and he was back in his fishing boat off the Baltic coast.

Captain Schneidewind was standing beside the helmsman. He stared through the big window at the darkness ahead. There was nothing to be seen but inky water. The deserted expanse of sea seemed to mirror his emotions. The night was chill, fraught with potential danger. He had an insidious sense of foreboding.

He turned away. The coffee he'd ordered would do him good. Maybe a bath. A clean shirt and a shave, too. His cabin was just below. He reached it and started to open the door.

Schwantke lowered his arm, signalling the torpedo officer to open fire.

He heard the firing-lever being depressed.

U43 gave three successive jolts as the bow torpedoes left their tubes. Schwantke pictured them speeding through the water, straight as arrows, three steel sharks with minds of their own, already beyond the power of anyone on earth to recall.

A voice behind him began counting the seconds to impact.

A muffled explosion shook the *Doggerbank*. Kuert knew at once what it meant. It wasn't a rational inference; there was no time for that. The electrical impulse reached his brain in a split second: torpedo! Instinctively, he dashed to the ladder and scrambled up the iron steps.

He heard someone shout 'Torpedo!' in his ear, then realized that the voice was his own, realized that he was yelling as he ran across the deck, blundering into dozens of other men who were desperately trying to reach the rail.

He hadn't gone more than a few yards when a second torpedo hit the *Doggerbank*, ripping her open amidships. The explosion sent him flying. He was showered with sea-water by the geyser that erupted alongside the ship and came pattering down on the deck.

He lay there for a moment, half-stunned. The ship's engines had stopped. She was losing way and developing a heavy list. Dim figures were staggering past him and jumping overboard.

The sight of them brought Kuert to his senses, dispelled

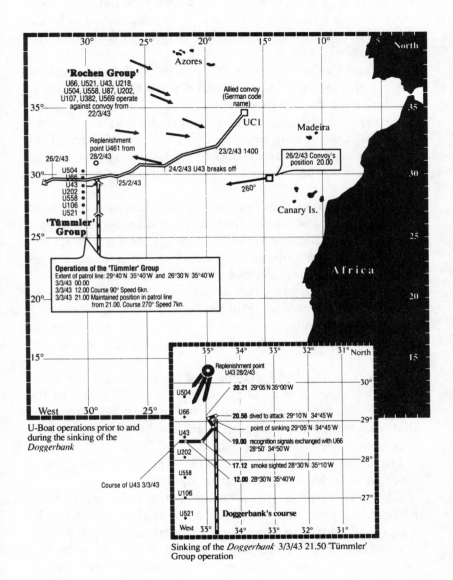

'Rochen Group'
U66, U521, U43, U218,
U504, U558, U87, U202,
U107, U382, U569 operate
against convoy from
22/3/43

Allied convoy
(German code
name)
UC1

Madeira

Azores

Replenishment
point U461 from
28/2/43

23/2/43 1400

26/2/43

U504
U66
U43
U202
U558
U106
U521

24/2/43 U43 breaks off

26/2/43 Convoy's
position 20.00

25/2/43

260°

Canary Is.

**'Tümmler'
Group**

Operations of the 'Tümmler' Group
Extent of patrol line: 29°40'N 35°40'W and 26°30'N 35°40'W
3/3/43 00.00
3/3/43 12.00 Course 90° Speed 6kn.
3/3/43 21.00 Maintained position in patrol line
from 21.00. Course 270° Speed 7kn.

Africa

West 30° 25°

U-Boat operations prior to and
during the sinking of the
Doggerbank

35° 34° 33° 32° 31° North

Replenishment point
U43 28/2/43

U504

20.21 29°05'N 35°00'W

U66

20.56 dived to attack 29°10'N 34°45'W

point of sinking 29°05'N 34°45'W

U43

19.00 recognition signals exchanged with U66
28°50'N 34°50'W

U202

17.12 smoke sighted 28°30'N 35°10'W

Course of U43 3/3/43

U558

12.00 28°30'N 35°40'W

U106

U521

Doggerbank's course

West 35° 34° 33° 32° 31°

Sinking of the *Doggerbank* 3/3/43 21.50 'Tümmler'
Group operation

the shock to his system, recalled a lesson drawn from past experience: the first to jump overboard seldom stood a chance; they were usually sucked down by the undertow. One's best aid to survival was the wreckage of a ship, the hatch covers, crates, and baulks of timber that floated to the surface when the vessel foundered. And then it occurred to him that one of his duties was to launch a lifeboat.

He crawled across the canting deck on his hands and knees. Terrified screams rang out near by. They grew louder. They were coming from Compartment No. 3, just abaft the bridge, where over a hundred men were accommodated in twin-tier bunks.

He saw it at once: the heavy iron ladders leading down to the 'tween-deck had come unshipped and cut off the men's escape. The compartment was in darkness except for a few pinpoints of light from some emergency lamps, but he had no need to see anything. The piercing cries for help, crazy with terror, were revealing enough. Hundreds of tons of water were pouring through rents in the hull, bulkhead doors bursting open, men trampling each other to death as they strove to escape the swiftly rising water that was imprisoning them in an iron tomb.

They hadn't a hope. There was no escape for the hundred men down there. They would drown like rats in the flooded compartment and go to the bottom with the ship that was inexorably dragging them down with her. There was nothing he could do for them.

He turned away and staggered on like a blind man. *I must get to my boat.* He clung to that thought.

The third torpedo struck the ship just as he reached the lifeboat, hanging from its davits at an angle dictated by the *Doggerbank*'s list. The retaining ropes were under such tension that he couldn't free the pins that held them. He wrenched an axe from its clips on the rail. Barely able to keep his feet by now, he hacked away wildly at the retaining ropes, but it was no use. The ropes were of steel, and it took him six blows to sever the first of them. He knew he would never free the boat, but he continued to hack away until he saw the ship's bow begin to rear up against the night sky. He threw the axe away. When he turned to look, the base of the mainmast was already awash. Aware that the end was near, he marvelled at his composure: not a trace of panic, just an overpowering determination to survive. The dinghy! Of course! They'd taken it aboard in Japan. It was there on the boat deck, and it wasn't lashed down!

The water almost overtook him, because he could already hear it gurgling close behind him as he reached the little craft. There was only one thing for it: he just had time to insert his hands in the loops of the grab-rope that ran round the hull.

Water engulfed the boat and the man clinging to it. The iron foremast shot towards them. Kuert felt the grab-rope cut into his wrists. The pain was intense, but his fear of being smashed against the mast was even greater. He might have let go if his hands hadn't been so firmly imprisoned. As it was, the mast flashed past like a knife, missing him by inches. His next conscious sensation was of being under water.

Everything went black. Something was constricting his chest, squeezing the breath out of him. His head threatened to burst. He couldn't feel his arms or legs. His limbs might have been torn from his body.

This is it! He found the prospect of death less terrifying than novel and wholly unfamiliar.

The undertow of the sinking ship sucked the dinghy down, and him with it, to a depth of some thirty feet. Recalling those moments in after life, he felt that there was only one thought which his fear of death had failed to suppress:

Hang on. Hang on to the dinghy. A boat will rise to the surface quicker than a man.

The pressure lessened as the dinghy shot to the surface like a cork. His limbs were suddenly restored to him. He removed his hands from the loops in the grab-rope. His wrists felt as if he had broken them. He got his arms over the gunwale and clung to it. His body heaved convulsively as he hung there, vomiting up the water he'd swallowed.

A strange silence surrounded him. The dinghy had righted itself and surfaced keel-down. It was full of water, but it floated nonetheless. He raised his head and peered into the darkness.

Their ship, their legendary, happy ship. It was like a dream, a dreadful hallucination: the *Doggerbank* had all but disappeared. Her bow pointed skyward, seemed to hang there for a moment, and slid beneath the surface with the inexorability of lead melting in a crucible.

Kuert could feel her dying ripples gently rock the water-logged dinghy as he scrambled over the gunwale and hauled himself aboard.

The night seemed less dark now; it had paled to a grey, nebulous twilight. The dinghy rode the long swell without a sound. He could hear no cries for help. The silence was strangely profound and all-enveloping.

His wrists were bleeding, lacerated by the rope that had bitten into them. He groped for a handkerchief, only to find that he was naked except for a singlet and a pair of silk underpants bought in Yokohama. His trousers, shoes and socks were gone, torn from his body.

The survival belt! It occurred to him only now that he wasn't wearing it. Why on earth not? Why had he left it on his bunk together with the canteen and clasp-knife? Hadn't the klaxon sounded? No, that was at noon. The U-boat! Schneidewind's announcement over the public address system, the exuberant atmosphere on board.

Suddenly his thoughts turned to the others. He listened intently, but the darkness and silence persisted. He might have been the sole survivor.

Knee-deep in water, he searched the dinghy from stem to stern. It had possessed a mast, a sail and a pair of oars, but there was no sign of them. Only the tiller and rudder remained.

You've got a boat. You're alive and you've got a boat. Everything else can wait.

He became aware of sounds for the first time. They steadily increased in volume. The pressure on his eardrums was easing.

He shook his head like a wet dog, and it was as if someone had removed plugs from his ears. From one moment to the next the darkness around him ceased to be hushed and lifeless. Voices and cries for help were audible on every side. He simply hadn't heard them before.

He cupped his hands to his mouth.

'Over here!' he shouted. 'Over here, I've got a boat!'

He felt proud of having a boat, proud but frightened of being alone in it.

Sometimes the voices sounded very close, sometimes they receded.

He went on calling until, at last, a figure swam out of the gloom. All he saw at first were two arms hooked over the gunwale.

'The bastards sank us!' said a voice.

'Careful,' he said, thinking clearly again. 'Climb in over the stern. We don't want to capsize.'

The face was thin and bloodless, the forehead plastered with strands of wet hair. He caught the glint of a couple of gold teeth.

'Is that you, Polack?' He wasn't sure. So many of his shipmates had gold teeth.

'Fritz, by God!' Stachnovski gasped. 'Fritz, you're alive!'

He'd lost his riding boots and his huntsman's jacket. His sodden shirt gaped open, revealing the fresh tattoo on his bare chest.

'How did you manage to get out?'

Stachnovski shook his head. 'Search me.' He went on shaking his head, but not at the fact of his survival. 'Christ, Fritz, what happened to the ship?' He peered into the darkness. 'My lovely ship.'

They huddled together in the stern sheets, each eyeing the other as if trying to see the reflection of his own face. Cries for help could be heard all around, some faint and distant, others closer at hand. Abruptly, Stachnovski straightened up. He glared into the darkness and shook his fist. It was a helpless, impotent gesture. 'How could the bastards do that to my ship!' He couldn't go on. His eyes were filled with tears.

U43 broke surface. Schwantke himself opened the upper hatch and came out on the bridge. The lookouts took up their posts around him. He levelled his night glasses.

The U-boat captain still retained a vivid picture of the ship's last moments as he had observed them through his periscope. Barely eight minutes had elapsed between the instant when she was almost obscured by the first huge waterspout and her final descent into the depths. Schwantke had watched the spectacle, fascinated. His first ship, his first kill. He was still surprised at how easy it had been, but still suspicious. He'd kept the site of the sinking under surveillance for an hour before giving the order to surface at 21.58, one hour past the time at which he'd been supposed to rejoin the rest of the 'Tümmler' Group. This presented a serious risk, because the expected convoy might well be heading through the gap occasioned by his absence. Although *U43* should have taken up its place in the patrol line without delay, Schwantke had other ideas.

'We'll take one more look,' he decreed.

U43 headed for the spot at slow speed. For a while nothing broke the silence but the throb of the submarine's diesel engines. Schwantke turned to the officer of the watch.

'We'd better try to confirm her name.'

U43 described a wide arc. The men on the bridge soon sighted some wreckage. The port lookout was the first to report. 'Men in the water at red two-zero, sir.' They were dead. They floated past at close range, face down in the water. Schwantke stopped engines and drifted.

Cries for help could be heard in the silence that followed.

'You speak a bit of English, Number One,' Schwantke told the officer of the watch. 'Get down on the fore-casing and question them. I want the name of their ship!'

The first officer had already started down the ladder when he paused. 'Shall we fish someone out?'

There was a long silence. Schwantke, leaning over the bridge casing, stared down at the water that had closed over his first and only kill. He had already taken a risk, chasing after an unescorted ship when his duty was to maintain station in the patrol line.

'Find out her name, that's all,' he said finally. 'We must be getting back.'

The two men in the dinghy had started to bail, but it was a hopeless task with their bare hands alone.

'We'll never get rid of the water like this,' Stachnovski said at last. 'What happened to the lifeboats?'

Kuert described his own abortive efforts.

'But what about the other three? Goddammit, one of them must have been launched. Those boats are stocked with food and water. We've got to find them, Fritz.'

Someone shouted for help near by. They shouted back and listened until they heard the sound of someone swimming. It was Waldemar Ring. The youngster burst out sobbing when they hauled him aboard. Like Kuert, he was only wearing his shirt and underpants. He'd jumped from the bridge, he told them eventually. Had he seen Schneidewind? Yes, he'd last seen the skipper emerging from his cabin, carrying a sea-bag. Ship's papers, probably.

'Well, go on.'

'That's all I know.' The sixteen-year-old was shivering with cold and shock. He looked scrawnier than ever. The eyes in his thin face conveyed a mute appeal, as though he expected them to reassure him that all would be well.

'We'll be okay,' Kuert told him firmly. 'We've got this boat. With a boat, we're laughing. Someone'll pick us up sooner or later.'

'The submarine, you mean? It was a submarine, wasn't it?'

The older men exchanged a silent glance. 'We'll see what's what when it gets light,' Kuert said. 'Someone's bound to pick us up when it gets light.' The words sounded ludicrously hollow, and he knew it. Did he believe them himself? It didn't matter what he believed. All that mattered was to do something. He turned to Stachnovski.

'You go up forward, Polack. There's plenty of flotsam

around. See if you can salvage something useful.'

'And look out for Leo!' Waldemar said eagerly. 'He jumped in after me, but I lost sight of him. Please!' When Stachnovski went forward the boy waded after him and cowered down in the bottom of the boat, waist-deep in water. Stachnovski leant out over the bow, scanning the surface.

Papa Boywitt came aboard soon afterwards. He'd been drifting on part of a hatch cover when he sighted the dinghy and paddled towards it.

Kuert helped him over the stern.

'Who is it?' Stachnovski called.

'Boywitt,' Kuert called back.

'It's all your fault, Papa,' said Stachnovski. 'You can't have been praying hard enough.'

Boywitt didn't reply. He had also lost his shoes and trousers, but he was still wearing his blue seaman's jacket with the brass buttons and his cap. He wrung it out before speaking.

'Where's the sail?'

'No sail, no mast, no oars, nothing,' Kuert replied, but Boywitt's presence reassured him. So did his prompt inquiry about the sail. Boywitt was a fisherman, an expert on small craft.

'First thing to do is get the water out of her.' Boywitt was calm personified.

'Sure, but how?'

Boywitt silently indicated his cap, which he'd managed to preserve. He proceeded to use it as a bailer.

It was good having Boywitt aboard, Kuert thought again. There was room in the dinghy for eight or nine men, but much would depend on who they were. If they hoped to survive they needed experienced, imperturbable types like Boywitt. He was probably the only one of them that knew the *Doggerbank*'s exact position when she went down and where to make for when it became light. The Baltic trawlerman was a good boat-handler.

While the *Doggerbank* was being refitted as a blockade-runner in the yard at Yokohama, some of the crew had been sent on leave to the mountain resort of Hakone. They were housed in a couple of lakeside bungalows, and Kuert had gone out on the water with Boywitt every day. They would get up at three in the morning, so no one beat them to the only available sailing dinghy. He, Kuert, had always thought he knew a lot about boat-handling, but Papa Boywitt had taught him a whole lot more.

Boywitt was still bailing with his cap when they came across the tarpaulin. Prevented from sinking by a bubble of trapped air, it drifted towards them like a big black jellyfish. It was a sizeable sheet, maybe fifteen square feet. They had some difficulty in hauling it into the boat, and Kuert had even greater difficulty in tearing the tough, tarred canvas with his bare hands. He managed to detach a piece some three feet square. Then, each holding two corners, he and Boywitt proceeded to use it as a bailer. Although it was more effective than Boywitt's cap, the dinghy was still half full after an hour's hard work.

They could hear Stachnovski cursing all the time. He kept fishing things out and throwing them back. 'Hell and damnation,' he would growl, 'still nothing edible!'

He was so obsessed with the thought of food that on one occasion they only just prevented him from jettisoning a length of rope.

'You expect me to eat that?'

'Nothing gets thrown away in this boat.' Kuert snatched the rope from his hands. 'Anything may come in handy, anything at all.'

Stachnovski continued to scan the surface and curse, but from now on he consulted them whenever he found something. 'A crate. Empty. Want it?'

He fished out an empty 105 mm. shell-case, miraculously bobbing in the sea open end up. It held around a gallon and made such an ideal bailer that they soon emptied the dinghy of the remaining water. Stachnovski's search yielded more lengths of rope and rope's ends. Then they found three oars in quick succession.

These could only have come from a lifeboat. Stachnovski

went wild with joy at the prospect of finding one, with its emergency transmitter and ample supply of food and water, but the oars were all they found. Of the lifeboats themselves they saw no sign.

Boywitt was wide awake at once. He stood one of the oars on end and inserted it experimentally in the hole in the dinghy's central thwart. It fitted.

'We'll take two oars,' he suggested, 'lash them together, and there's our mast. The other one we can use as a spar, and the tarp will make a sail. No point in hanging around.'

Kuert nodded. He was gladder than ever to have Boywitt on board.

Now that the boat was higher in the water they could hear the gentle, persistent lapping of the water against its sides as it rode the swell. But Kuert was conscious of another sound as well. He cocked his head and listened. It was a faint hum reminiscent of a diesel engine. The submarine? The sound died away. He couldn't be certain, so he refrained from saying anything.

He got the ropes and the tarpaulin ready.

'Right,' he said, 'let's get started.'

U43's first officer was still down on the fore-casing. Schwantke couldn't see him clearly from the bridge, but he could hear him calling.

'What ship? What ship are you?'

The cries for help issuing from the gloom seemed to be growing louder. Schwantke thought he identified the language as English.

How many of the *Doggerbank*'s 365 men had survived the torpedoing and sinking of their ship? The precise number will never be known, but it is probable that about one-third of them were still alive at this juncture and could have been saved. However, no one in *U43* seemed to doubt that the ship in question was British.

The first officer continued to hail the survivors from his post on the fore-casing.

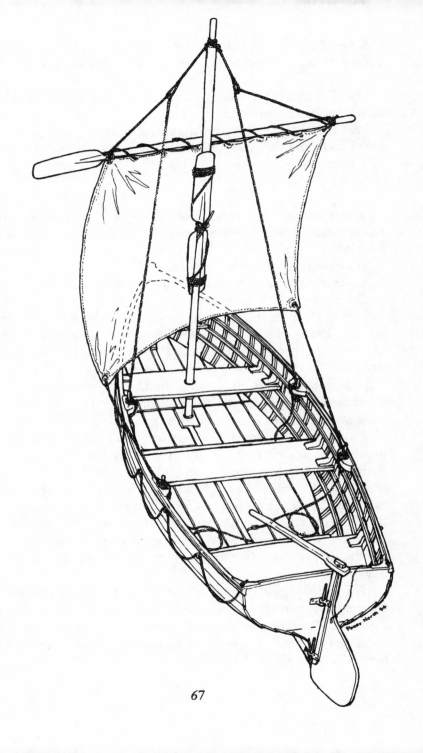

A piece of wreckage struck the outer hull with a dull thud. 'Hurry it up,' Schwantke called, 'we've got to get back!'

The first officer climbed back up the conning tower. 'Well,' said Schwantke, 'any luck?'

The first officer shrugged. 'Nothing definite, skipper. I heard someone shout something. Could have been the name of a British ship.'

'The *Dunedin Star*?' That was the only clue to date, the resemblance between their victim and and the type in Lloyd's Register.

'I couldn't say for sure.'

Another piece of flotsam nudged the hull.

The cries for help grew louder.

'Life-raft on the port beam, sir!' one of the lookouts reported. 'Pretty big, quite a few men aboard.' His voice rose. 'A couple of them have dived in! They're swimming towards us. Can't be more than twenty metres away!'

Schwantke gave an order, and the U-boat went astern. As it left the wreckage and the life-raft behind, Schwantke looked back at the site of the sinking through his night glasses.

Why hadn't he picked someone up? There were no formal instructions against doing so. Only one day later *U515* sank a British ship south of the Azores and ascertained her name by picking up her chief engineer. Why not Schwantke, especially as it was dark and his boat was in no danger of detection from the air? *U43*'s war diary expressly states that Schwantke was afraid the wreckage would foul his propellers, but that seems a dubious pretext. His conduct remains inexplicable to this day.

U43 rejoined the 'Tümmler' Group at 10.30. Its immediate neighbour in the patrol line, *U66*, flashed a recognition signal. *U43* acknowledged the signal in kind and reported its success. The response came flickering through the darkness: CONGRATULATIONS.

PART TWO

THE BOAT

1. Fritz Kuert, sole survivor of the *Doggerbank*, after his release from an American prisoner-of-war camp in January, 1945.

2. Fritz Kuert's parents with their new-born son in 1918.

3. Fritz Kuert at the age of six.

4. Fritz Kuert at the helm of the *Brake* in 1938.

5. Fritz Kuert as boatswain of the *Charlotte Schliemann* at Las Palmas in 1942.

6. Fritz Kuert's children, Karin, Fred and Brunhilde.

They'd been hard at it all night. By the time the grey light of dawn washed over them, the makeshift sail was ready. Boywitt hauled the square of tarred canvas up the mast. Then they waited in the cool of the morning for a breeze to spring up.

Kuert had taken the tiller, Boywitt handled the ropes that would enable him to work the sail. It was on the large side for such a small boat, and they quickly picked up speed once the wind came.

'We're sailing!' Kuert exclaimed. 'My God, Papa, we're sailing!' He bent down and called to Stachnovski under the sail. 'Keep an eye open for wreckage, Polack. Maybe we'll come across some of the others.'

But there was no wreckage in sight. Being higher in the water and more exposed to wind, they had probably drifted further during the night than any flotsam from the ship. There was nothing around them now but sea, a grey expanse illuminated by the eerie half-light in the east. The clouds hung low, as leaden grey as the water beneath.

The feel of the tiller was a comfort. Kuert was far from down-hearted. Whenever he was assailed by memories of the sinking, he suppressed them and concentrated on the present. He had weathered the night's ordeal remarkably well. It surprised him how little he felt the cold.

I'm in good shape. I've been sunk before now with plenty less flesh on my bones. I'm well fed and well rested. They really set me up, those months of idleness in Japan.

He looked down at his broad chest and muscular arms. He was at his optimum weight, 180 pounds. It annoyed him not to be wearing his survival belt, but he wasn't seriously concerned.

The wind strengthened, the sky grew paler by the minute. Boywitt studied the clouds. 'I reckon the wind'll hold,' he said.

'Easy!' called Stachnovski. Some crates and hatch covers were drifting past. He pointed ahead. 'Look! Over there, a bit to starboard. Are they alive?'

Kuert, who had already spotted the bobbing heads, steered in their direction. He counted seven of them, all floating face down. Nothing could be seen of the men but their life-jackets and their hair, which had fanned out like fine seaweed.

He took the boat in closer. Leaning over the gunwale, he grasped a life-jacket and lifted the limp head clear of the water. The face was draped with wet, fair hair. He gave a start of horror and let go at once, but not before recognition had dawned.

Boywitt raised a hand and touched his forehead, chest and shoulders in turn. His lips moved as he crossed himself.

Kuert swallowed hard. 'Kordes,' he said, 'that was Kordes.' He put the tiller over and sheered off. His mind's eye conjured up the dead man as he had been only last night, before the sinking, seated on his bunk with the suitcase beside him. He could still see Kordes exchanging his last few pairs of canvas shoes for smokes, still see the open suitcase overflowing with packets of R6 cigarettes.

They found more dead bodies, but they made no attempt to identify them. They also found four survivors.

The first to be hauled aboard by Stachnovski was the gunner's mate, Gernhöfer, a man in his forties. He was naked except for a shirt and in the last stages of exhaustion.

Next came Klockmann, the officers' steward. Only just twenty, Klockmann was a hefty young fellow who thought nothing of shouldering a veal calf from the cold store and climbing a ladder with it, so he was little the worse for his night in the water. The last two to be fished out were Bergmann, an engineer apprentice, and Lofty Hencke, the helmsman.

None of them had seen any of the lifeboats, and none knew what had become of the skipper.

The little craft rode lower in the water with eight men on board. They had stripped off whatever they were wearing in the way of shirts and jackets, wrung them out, and draped them over the gunwale to dry. The sun, which now came out, was a welcome sight. An hour went by. No wreckage, no more dead bodies or survivors, just open sea. Kuert tried to read what was in the others' eyes and interpret their demeanour. *Eight men. We can pick up another three or four at most.* And then? There was only one thing for it: they must make for the nearest land. But where was it? He tried to visualize the map, the coastlines and island groups, but all he saw was a broad, deserted expanse of sea.

He leant towards Boywitt and lowered his voice so the others wouldn't hear. 'Know anything about navigation?'

Boywitt looked down at his hands, which were holding the rope attached to the sail. 'Not enough to make an accurate landfall.'

'At least we've got the boat.'

'Only the skipper would know enough.'

Stachnovski crawled aft beneath the sail. His face, thin enough at the best of times, was a hollow-cheeked shadow of its former self. Immersion in sea-water had inflamed the fresh tattoo on his chest, Kuert noticed.

'Reckon there's still a hope of finding one of the lifeboats?' he asked.

'Yes, if they managed to launch one.'

'And if not?'

'Don't be a pessimist, Polack. You always wanted to grow a beard. Now's your chance.'

But Stachnovski refused to be cajoled. 'You know what this means, don't you? We're done for, Fritz. Not a bite to eat, not a drop of drinking water, nothing. We might as well . . . '

Kuert cut him short. 'Get back to your place,' he said. 'And give your brains a rest. It doesn't do to think too much, not in a situation like this.'

I ought to know.

None of the others had experienced a sinking before. He had, more than once. He'd seen so many men die that he was under no illusion about their predicament, but one thing he knew for sure: thinking was poison. It sapped your strength.

Keep your eyes open, remain alert by all means, but don't think, or, if you do, no more than a minute ahead.

'The sub!' The voice was that of Stachnovski, crouching at his lookout's post in the bow. 'I saw its periscope!' He pointed into the sun, and for a moment Kuert yielded to the same delusion. He was incapable of speech or movement.

'It's a life-raft,' Papa Boywitt said eventually. They could all see it clearly now: one of the *Doggerbank*'s big inflatables was wallowing in the swell. What Stachnovski had mistaken for a periscope was merely an oar with a shirt fluttering on the end.

Kuert steered for it until he could see over the life-raft's bulbous sides and make out the figures, at least thirty of them, huddled together on the bottom. Another thirty or forty men were in the water, hanging on to the grab-rope.

Kuert put the helm up when the dinghy came to within a hundred metres or so. Boywitt gave him a look of inquiry.

'If they all decide to make a dash for it, they'll capsize us,' Kuert said. 'We'll stay within hailing distance.'

'The skipper!' Stachnovski yelled. 'He made it! He's there on board!'

Kuert thought he glimpsed Schneidewind's white cap and blue tunic. Cautiously, he brought the dinghy in closer.

'Who's in charge?' It was Schneidewind's voice right enough.

'Boatswain Kuert, sir!' The words came out quite naturally, although Papa Boywitt was older.

'How many of you?'

'Eight.'

'Seen any lifeboats?'

'We've looked everywhere. Not a sign of them.'

There was silence for a while. Then Schneidewind called, 'We've got to find a boat. This thing's leaking, and there are too many of us. Go on looking and stay in touch!'

Kuert stared across at the white cap. He wasn't thinking of the rest, only that they needed a man capable of navigating in mid-ocean. After his own experience with the lifeboat he felt

74

almost certain that none of the other boats had got away. There simply hadn't been time. But that wasn't his present concern.

Leaning forwards, he cupped his hands around his mouth. 'We need a navigator, sir. How about sending an officer across?'

They could see the men in the life-raft debating this suggestion. Then Schneidewind's voice carried to them on the breeze.

'Very well. Lieutenant Fischer will join you.'

'Not Fischer!' Stachnovski protested in a low voice. 'Keep that madman off our backs, Fritz. He'll have us all standing at attention and saluting!'

Kuert looked at the others one by one, and one by one they shook their heads. He made another megaphone out of his hands.

'How about joining us yourself, Captain? Maybe we'll find a lifeboat quicker that way.'

He kept his eyes glued to the life-raft, poised to sheer off at a moment's notice. He could see a couple of men operating the pumps.

'Very well,' Schneidewind called at last, 'stand by to pick me up.'

Kuert saw him climb over the side and lower himself into the water. 'Polack, get ready to grab him.' He gave Boywitt a nudge. 'Stand by to sheer off.'

The two craft were only some twenty metres apart by now. Schneidewind struck out for the dinghy and Stachnovski hauled him aboard. Kuert put the tiller hard over and the others ducked as the sail flapped and filled again.

Practice makes perfect, Kuert told himself proudly. Besides, their chances were even better now they had the skipper on board.

Schneidewind seated himself in the stern and took the helm. He was still in his sodden uniform, the only man on board to be fully clothed. He looked up at the sail, then at his eight companions. For a moment his lips pursed in a wry smile, but it vanished as soon as he saw Kuert looking at him.

'What happened to your lifeboat, Kuert? How come you didn't manage to launch it?'

Kuert had relinquished his place at the helm and was seated facing Boywitt in the bottom of the boat.

'No time, sir. I tried, but the list was too extreme.' He avoided mentioning the submarine or inquiring about it.

'And you didn't see what became of the others?'

'I doubt if they got away either.'

'We'll take another look,' Schneidewind said. 'There are over seventy men in and around that life-raft, and it's leaking badly. They're pumping in relays, four men a time, but the water's gaining. They may last the day, but not another night.'

He removed his uniform tunic. Boywitt took it from him and hung it up to dry. His dark blue rollneck sweater was also soaking wet, but he made a dismissive gesture: it would dry on his body. He surveyed the others.

'Did any of you see the submarine?'

They all shook their heads in turn. No one spoke.

'Some of the fellows on the life-raft said they saw it,' Schneidewind went on, 'last night, after the sinking. Binder was there.' Richard Binder was one of the *Doggerbank*'s helmsmen. 'He said they swam towards it and shouted for help. According to him, someone aboard the submarine asked the name of the ship – in English.'

Stachnovski emitted a Silesian oath. Schneidewind was clearly reluctant to talk about the submarine.

'Did they pick anyone up?' Kuert asked.

'Binder says no. They got to within a few yards of the boat, but as soon as they were spotted it backed off.'

The wind freshened and the dinghy put on speed. Schneidewind devoted his attention to the tiller.

They quartered the area all day long, coming across widely scattered pieces of wreckage and more seaweed-haired bodies floating face-down in life-jackets, their owners having drowned or died of exhaustion and exposure. They found no lifeboats, but eventually, when the light had already begun to fade, they sighted a raft from the *Doggerbank*.

The clumsy craft consisted of a wooden deck supported by two big galvanized drums that kept it well clear of the water. Perched on the deck were Henry Schaper, one of the ship's engineers, a stoker named Thielmann, and, unnoticed until Waldemar Ring gave a sudden shout, Leo, the ship's dog.

The grey fox-terrier leapt into the dinghy and on to Waldemar's lap, where it whimpered and licked his face before cowering between his legs.

Schaper and Thielmann clambered aboard and, on Schneidewind's instructions, took the raft in tow. There was room on it for a good twenty men, so it held out the prospect of safety for at least some of those in the life-raft.

Darkness was falling fast and the dinghy made little headway with the bulky raft in tow. Although Schneidewind reckoned that they must be in the vicinity of the life-raft, they sailed far into the night without making contact. They shouted repeatedly, taking it in turns to conserve their strength, but there was no response.

Schneidewind eventually abandoned the search. Boywitt lowered the sail and they drifted with the two craft made fast to each other so that the dinghy lay in the lee of the raft.

The wind had strengthened. This was their second night in the open, and Kuert, who had retained his place beside the skipper, was feeling the cold for the first time.

The other nine were stretched out in the bottom of the boat with the remainder of the tarpaulin over them. Adjusting their position uncomfortably from time to time, they lay huddled close together for warmth on the hard wooden ribs.

Around them were the noises of the night, the incessant slap of the waves against the hollow drums supporting the raft, the occasional cough or muffled curse of a man stirring in his sleep, the monotonous murmur of Boywitt saying his prayers.

Kuert dozed with his head propped on his knees, shivering in the icy wind, shivering, too, because of something unrelated to the chill of the night: an unspoken realization of their true predicament.

Whenever he looked up he could see the skipper seated

motionless in the stern. Schneidewind was back in his uniform tunic. The brass buttons gleamed, the white cap caught the fitful moonlight that bathed one side of his face.

Schneidewind remained awake all night. He sat there stiffly, erect and alert, waiting for daybreak, and Kuert waited with him.

The morning of the second day after the sinking was as bleak and depressing as the night had been. The sea was rougher. The eleven men in the dinghy awoke one by one, stiff-limbed and shivering with cold. They looked in silence at the flecks of white foam on the waves, the grey sky overhead.

It was Schneidewind who roused and heartened them.

'Look lively! We've got to find that life-raft.'

Boywitt raised the sail, and they got under way with the heavy raft in tow. They made even slower progress than the day before, thanks to the waves that were buffeting them about.

There was still no sign of the life-raft an hour later, but Stachnovski was the first to sight a sprinkling of black dots alternately bobbing on the wave-crests and buried in the intervening troughs. Schneidewind made in their direction. When the dinghy drew nearer, they proved to be the heads of several swimmers battling desperately against the heavy sea.

'Four,' Kuert counted. 'Only four of them.' They were near enough now for their faces to be recognizable. 'I can see Binder, and Bahrend.'

Schneidewind, sitting motionless at the helm, was unable to repress a momentary look of dismay.

'My God!' He breathed the words almost inaudibly. 'My God, they were with me in the life-raft. Only four of them?' They scanned the sea for more survivors, but in vain.

The four were hauled aboard one by one: Binder, an able seaman with a balding head that belied his twenty years; Heller, nineteen, another of the naval ratings transferred to the *Doggerbank* at Yokohama; Schuster, also little more than nineteen, a slim, silent youth whose parents had been killed in an air raid on Leipzig; and Jan Bahrend, the ex-cook. They lay in the bottom of the boat, utterly exhausted, with grey, gaunt faces from which the realization that they were safe had not yet banished the horror of what they had been through.

Kuert bent over Bahrend and looked into his salt-inflamed eyes. He gripped him by the shoulders and shook him gently. 'What happened?'

Stachnovski said, 'At least we won't be bored now, not with our prize yarn-spinner aboard.' His tone was jocular, but his voice trembled as he spoke.

'What happened?' Kuert repeated. Bahrend brushed the question aside with a gesture so pathetically weary and resigned that it tugged at Kuert's heart. He pointed to Binder. 'Ask him. He'll tell you.'

'What happened to the life-raft?' Schneidewind demanded.

'It's gone,' Binder said haltingly.

'How do you mean?'

'Last night. Someone said you'd pushed off and left us in the lurch. That started it.' Binder buried his face in his hands. He'd been renowned on board for his laugh – and his sisters. There were six of them, and Binder was always on the lookout for likely husbands. This time he'd found two candidates whom he intended to take on leave with him and introduce to the said sisters. He had photographs of them, pretty girls all. They were his bargaining counter, so to speak. 'Hand over your cigarette ration and you can be my brother-in-law!' That was his usual pitch, accompanied by a high-pitched, almost girlish laugh. No one had known how seriously to take him.

'The men at the pumps gave up,' he went on. 'They said it was pointless. A few of the others, the ones in the water, let go and drifted away. Then Fischer shot himself.'

Schneidewind seemed to have aged ten years. He looked an old, beaten man. 'He had a gun?'

Binder nodded. 'An automatic. It was in a waterproof pouch round his neck.'

Schneidewind's hand went to his chest. Kuert noticed the

instinctive movement but gave it no particular thought at the time.

'Well, go on,' Schneidewind said.

'It was Fischer that set them off. The men around him must have got hold of his gun. They went crazy. We heard eight shots.'

Schneidewind's expressionless face was a mask, a form of self-protection. He shut his eyes for a moment as though insulating himself against reality. Then he surveyed the little boat and his fourteen companions, all that remained of the three hundred and sixty-five who had sailed from Yokohama.

'We all lost our heads after that,' Binder went on. 'Everyone panicked. Some jumped in and swam off rather than prolong the agony. The rest of us stayed aboard the liferaft, but it didn't take long to sink with no one working the pumps.'

'And you're the sole survivors?' Schneidewind asked.

'We were the only ones with life-jackets. Everyone else must be dead by now.'

An almost unnatural silence descended on the boat. All eyes turned to Schneidewind, every face registered a mixture of dread and foreboding. The others' death was suddenly forgotten, unreal. They were afraid for themselves. Did *they* stand a chance?

They continued to look at the skipper. There was only one certainty now: the deep respect and absolute confidence he had always inspired in them. Bereft of everything else, they clung to it in their hour of need.

Their concerted gaze seemed to galvanize him. 'Look in your pockets, all of you,' he said, but it was useless. They had nothing on them but the remains of their clothing, not even a shred of tobacco.

'There's only one thing for it,' Schneidewind said eventually. 'We must make for land.'

They stared at him. Fifteen men in a dinghy with barely a foot of freeboard, they were not only hundreds of miles from land; they had no compass, no food, no drinking water.

Once more, their faces reflected the hopelessness of their predicament.

'We're nearer the Azores than anywhere else,' Schneidewind went on, 'but our chances of getting there are nil. We'd have the prevailing wind against us. Besides, it's colder in the north. The Azores are out.'

The sun pierced the clouds for moments at a time, but it gave little warmth.

'The Bahamas? Too far north. Without a centreboard we can only sail about five points off the wind.' Schneidewind fell silent. Finally, as if his mind had been made up from the outset, he said, 'Our only hope is South America.'

They stared at each other, at the boat, at the sea. South America? It sounded a preposterous idea.

'In this cockleshell?' Stachnovski demanded. 'With nothing to eat? Without any water?'

'It won't be easy,' Schneidewind said, 'but we'll have a following wind, and it's better to try than do nothing.'

'How long will it take?' Kuert asked.

'Our route will take us across at least seven neutral shipping lanes. Besides, the further south we go the warmer it'll get. Three weeks, if all goes well.'

Three weeks in this dinghy, thought Kuert, but all he said was, 'What about the raft, sir?'

The raft was wallowing alongside like a secure little island, virtually unsinkable even in the most violent of storms. All fifteen of them could easily have found room on board. It was a diabolical decision, and Kuert felt glad it wasn't his to make.

'We'll have to set it adrift,' Schneidewind decreed. 'We wouldn't make more than three knots with that dead weight in tow, and we've got to sail as fast and as far as we can.'

He inserted a hand in the pocket of his uniform tunic. It emerged holding a silver-sided pocket-knife. 'Preserve the towrope, Kuert. You never know when it may come in handy.'

Kuert hauled the raft in close. The knife had only one blade, and it was blunt by the time he had severed the rope. He sharpened it on one of the metal rowlock fittings.

The men in the dinghy watched in silence as the raft drifted away and dwindled to a speck amid the grey, heaving waves.

'You keep it,' Schneidewind told Kuert when he made to return the knife.

Kuert's hand closed over it. The feel of the knife gave him a curious sense of satisfaction: he possessed something denied to everyone else on board.

The raft had drifted out of sight.

'Two men stand by to bail,' Schneidewind ordered. 'Stachnovski and Hencke, you kick off. The rest of you distribute your weight evenly. Lie down in the bottom of the boat. You'll be warmer that way. Keep still and try to sleep. Save your strength.' He gave Boywitt a nod.

Boywitt raised the sail, Schneidewind took the helm.

It was midday, forty hours after *Doggerbank* went down, when her skipper brought the dinghy on course.

Kuert sat at Schneidewind's feet in the stern sheets. The space was so cramped that his knees brushed those of Boywitt, who was sitting opposite him.

His sense of satisfaction at having the knife persisted. So he'd lost yet another ship and this wasn't the Mediterranean. So he didn't have his survival belt and the dinghy was overladen, granted, but the skipper knew his stuff and he himself possessed a knife.

He cut two notches in the gunwale, one for each day, and put the crumbs of wood in his mouth. He chewed them slowly. That was something else the others didn't have.

The wind had strengthened still more. They were sailing with it and the current. Although the sun appeared from time to time, the air remained chill.

Kuert relieved Boywitt at the sail every two hours. The bailers, who sat beside the mast, were also relieved at two hourly intervals. Schneidewind alone retained his place at the tiller. The tension had left his face, which now wore a calm and confident expression. The decision had been taken, their course was set, the die cast. He could do no more.

Darkness fell. The slap of the waves against the sides of the boat and the creak of the makeshift rigging took on an eerie note.

'Take over, Kuert,' Schneidewind said at last.

Kuert cautiously slid into position on the stern seat and took the helm. He glanced at the sail.

'The sail stays up,' Schneidewind decreed. 'We must be making six or seven knots in this wind, but we'll have to keep going night and day.'

The sky, which had cleared, was frosted over with stars.

'See the Great Bear, Kuert?' Schneidewind pointed over his right shoulder. 'Always keep it five to ten degrees abaft the starboard beam.' Schneidewind's voice was calm and composed. 'Then we can't go wrong.'

We'd be in a real hole without the skipper, Kuert thought. He grasped the tiller with one hand and felt for the knife, which he'd rolled up in the elastic waistband of his underpants. He thought again how good it was to have something all to himself.

You've always been a lucky bastard. You'll make it all right.

Kuert cut another notch in the gunwale, the third. Schneidewind had relieved him at the tiller as soon as dawn broke, Boywitt was handling the sail.

The others stirred and sat up, but one look at the overcast sky sent them back into the relative warmth of the tarpaulin. There were periodic growls of protest: 'Shift your butt!' or 'Don't spread yourself so much!'

Whenever Kuert wasn't at the helm he tried to sleep, but hunger proved stronger than fatigue. His head emptied of all else when he thought of food. He thought of home and the piece of rented land behind the collier's house at Lünen where his parents lived. That was where he had grown up, in the shadow of the colliery. Like every miner, his father kept a pig and a few rabbits. Kuert could see the sides of pork now, suspended by their sinews from a wooden frame propped against the smoke-blackened plaster wall. His mother was in the wash-house, heating water in the copper. He could smell herbs, especially thyme. The vision swam before his eyes. Hunger was gnawing at his entrails. He was incapable of focusing his thoughts. The pig, for instance, why couldn't he see it any more? Why couldn't he smell that seething, greasy, herb-laden broth? His whole body was crying out for something to eat.

Neither Boywitt nor Schneidewind spoke. He could distinctly hear their stomachs rumbling, but they didn't utter a word. He wondered how much longer his pride would prevail over his hunger. He had an irresistible urge to tell them about the pig. He bit his lip. Surely it wouldn't be long before someone started talking about food? He guessed it would be Stachnovski. What culinary day-dream was the ever-ravenous Polack indulging in?

It was, in fact, Jan Bahrend who first broached the subject of food. He sat with his back propped against the mast, his favourite, jealously guarded spot, perhaps because he was as proud of it as Kuert of his knife. He sat there with a silk shirt under his life-jacket and his chef's sweat-rag round his neck. In his underpants when they fished him out, he had badgered young Heller, the only one aboard to have preserved his trousers apart from Stachnovski and the skipper, into 'selling' them to him for an exorbitant sum to be paid as soon as circumstances permitted. Bahrend was particular about his appearance even now; he couldn't bear to be seen in his underpants.

Bahrend's dissertation roused the others from their lethargy. He lectured them on spring chicken *à la turque*, stuffed turkey, duck with melon. He recounted where he'd sampled those dishes, where the finest birds were to be found, how they were prepared.

'Hey, Fritz, remember that steak we had at the New Grand? Remember that whole fillet they brought on a wooden board and carved in front of us? Sonofabitch, you didn't even need a knife to cut it. The meat was so tender it melted in your mouth! You know why? Because it was bullock's meat! Beer and massage, that's the secret. The Japs rear their bullocks on beer and massage them gently every day. Ah, those thick slices of tender, rosy, juicy steak.'

Even as he listened to Bahrend, Kuert knew it was a mistake to let him go on. It would only aggravate their hunger, making it more agonizing and harder to bear, but he listened avidly just the same.

Even Stachnovski was reduced to silence. He didn't curse or interrupt in any way.

Looking back on it later, Kuert decided that hunger was his worst torment in the three days that followed, the third, fourth and fifth days after the sinking, far worse even than thirst. It was on the morning of the fifth day – at least there were now five notches in the gunwale – that hunger very nearly overturned the boat.

At dawn Stachnovski crept up on Waldemar Ring and tried to wrest the dog away from him, cursing and shouting at the top of his voice. Waldemar not only resisted fiercely but ended by biting him. Stachnovski let out a yell of pain. The boat gave a perilous lurch as Hencke snatched up a heavy shackle and bore down on him. Kuert was just in time to separate them.

Stachnovski stared down at the blood oozing from his bitten hand and swore loudly. Hencke had turned pale. He dropped the shackle.

'I'd have killed him, Fritz,' he muttered to Kuert. 'I really would!'

Waldemar, still nursing Leo in his arms, was crouching in the bottom of the boat.

'That dog's no use to anyone,' Stachnovski snarled. 'It's in worse shape than we are.'

Kuert stared at him. This wasn't Polack speaking, not the man who'd always been so proud of his ship and his shipmates.

'What's the good of it?' Stachnovski insisted. 'I say we butcher the brute. We could drink its blood.'

Kuert had a momentary feeling that Stachnovski might be right, but the notion appalled him. He wondered how he could ever have entertained it.

'There's nothing on that dog but skin and bone,' said Hencke. 'Let's butcher Stachnovski instead. Hands up those in favour!'

For an instant no one knew if he really meant it. Stachnovski cowered away. His eyes widened, and he raised his hands defensively.

Kuert gripped him by the shoulders.

'Come on, Polack!' he entreated. 'What's the matter with you? Don't give up. We'll all be done for if we don't pull together.'

Stachnovski emitted a sudden laugh, a despairing, half-demented bark of laughter. 'Jan had better stop it, that's all. I can't stand it when he goes on about food.'

There was no more talk of food from Bahrend. The incident seemed quickly forgotten, but a change had come over the dinghy's occupants. They weren't the same men. It was as if each of them had crossed an invisible barrier beyond which different laws prevailed.

Schneidewind, still wearing his captain's white peaked cap, sat at the helm. He had taken no apparent notice of the dog incident and passed no comment on it, as if it were none of his business. All his mute attention was focused on the clouds, the sail and the sea.

It was a mystery where he found the strength. He seemed less weary and more alert than the rest. Hour after hour he sat there, seldom relinquishing the tiller to anyone else. He might have ceased to be a man and become an instrument sensitive to any change in the wind and current.

The weather steadily deteriorated. Waves broke over the dinghy, deluging its occupants with spray. They had to bail incessantly in teams of two, relieving each other every half hour because that was the limit of their endurance. The others huddled together beneath the tarpaulin, wet and shivering.

Schneidewind refused to take in sail. He headed straight on

through the storm until even Boywitt counselled caution. The skipper's only response was a shake of the head.

And that was how they passed the night and the following day and night, sailing and bailing, bailing and sailing. . .

The wind dropped at dawn on the seventh day. The sky was heavily overcast, and from time to time they sighted dark curtains of rain descending in the distance. Awakened by Stachnovski, the men had spread the tarpaulin in the bow in readiness to collect it. For hours the clouds rolled on ahead of them, fraught with promise, but by noon they seemed as far away as ever.

The men had long since abandoned all dignity. They gazed longingly at the clouds and whimpered for water. Their faces were pallid, their eyes sunken, their lips cracked and swollen. Watching the others, Kuert wondered vaguely if he looked like them.

It was not until nightfall that deliverance came. They sailed into a heavy downpour. Even while the rain was filling the tarpaulin, the men plunged their faces in it and drank like horses at a trough.

Hencke stood there with his face upturned, one hand gripping the mast and the other above his head. 'More!' he yelled as though invoking the heavens. 'Go on! Go on, more!'

Kuert had lowered the sail. There was no need for words: unbidden, Boywitt helped him to rinse the salt-encrusted canvas and collect some rain. Then he drank, gulping down great mouthfuls of it. When he paused to catch his breath, he became aware that the men around him were groaning with delight.

He drank till his belly was bulging. But, no sooner had he changed places with Schneidewind than he was suddenly terrified that the rain would stop before he could take another drink. He lusted after water until his whole body shook. Why was the skipper taking so long? What if the rain really did stop too soon?

He darted forward as soon as Schneidewind resumed his place in the stern. While drinking the first time he'd noticed nothing; this time he actually tasted the water. The tarred canvas lent it an odd flavour, but who cared? Who could tell when it would rain again?

He filled the shell-case and stowed it under the stern seat. Then, with the remainder of the fresh water in the sail, he sluiced his face and the suppurating weals on his wrists, which had never healed.

They set sail again and Schneidewind brought the dinghy back on course. The rain had soaked them all to the skin. At first, Kuert had found it a gloriously refreshing sensation; now, all he felt was the cold. And after an hour his thirst returned.

The dingy was plunging and rolling in a heavy sea. Early that morning – it was the eighth day, and another gale had blown up – Kuert distributed the water. Everyone got some, even the dog. The shell-case was half-empty by the time it had gone the rounds.

Watching the others as they drank, Kuert wondered again how closely he resembled them.

Stachnovski was very quiet now. He never swore, much as Kuert would have liked to hear him do so. Bahrend, too, had lapsed into silence. His flow of anecdotes had dried up. The inveterate pessimist and yarn-spinner just sat there in a stupor with his back propped against the mast. He didn't even duck when the heavy seas lashed his face with spindrift.

Kuert had noticed an odd thing a couple of nights ago. It was the smell that first attracted his attention, a faint whiff of lemons. He thought it was a figment of his imagination until he spotted something in Schneidewind's hand: a small tube of glycerine ointment from a first-aid kit. After that he kept watch every night. The skipper would squeeze out a little of the tube's contents and rub it into his face. He repeated this ritual night after night. Although Kuert felt as if he'd caught him engaging in some illicit activity, he couldn't tear his eyes away.

Perhaps the others, too, had little secrets of their own, things they divulged to no one else on board. He, for example, had his knife and the fragments of wood he carved out and chewed. Shouldn't he have shared his secret, shouldn't he have given a little crumb of wood to Boywitt? He did no such thing.

They no longer spoke to each other. Each was alone, enclosed in a strange cocoon of silence. They seemed to have forgotten that they had once sailed together in a ship named the *Doggerbank*. They had forgotten the war, the submarine, even, perhaps, the past. Stachnovski, who was Stachnovski? Just a name, nothing more. And Boywitt? He'd once known something about Boywitt, but he couldn't remember what. Come to that, who was he himself, Fritz Kuert?

He counted the notches, ran his finger over them. Five and three, eight in all. Eight notches. That meant today was, yes, Sunday. They'd been in the boat for a week.

Schneidewind had said it would get warmer. To Kuert it felt colder. Schneidewind had said they would cross some shipping lanes, but they hadn't sighted a single ship.

He experienced a sudden pang of doubt. Would he fail to stay the course? Even to consider such a possibility was crazy, the beginning of the end. The thought was draining his last reserves of energy. He thrust it aside.

At nightfall he took over the helm from Schneidewind. Till now he'd always done so without a word, but this time he spoke. It surprised him how normal his voice sounded.

'How far do you think we've come, sir?'

Schneidewind replied without hesitation. 'Eight hundred miles, by my reckoning. Maybe a bit more. We should soon be crossing the Tropic of Cancer.' He spoke as if it were a visible landmark.

'Are we half-way there yet?' Not for the first time, Kuert wondered where the skipper got his quiet confidence. What was his secret source of supply? Could it be that little tube of glycerine ointment? The scent of lemons?

'Not quite.'

One of the bailers beside the mast turned his head. Kuert couldn't identify him in the gloom. Not wanting to be overheard, he lowered his voice.

'What are our chances, sir?'

'Remember what I told you about the Great Bear,' Schneidewind said. He had lowered his voice too. 'Always keep it a few degrees abaft the starboard beam. Remember that, Kuert, just in case.'

There was silence for a while. Schneidewind hadn't really answered the question, he'd evaded it.

'I keep wondering,' he went on. 'I ask myself, time and time again, if it was my fault. That submarine, Kuert, I was so certain it was one of ours.'

'It must have been, mustn't it?'

'Maybe I was too damned certain.' Schneidewind's lips compressed themselves into a hard line.

Kuert saw it now: the skipper's composure was just a façade. Behind it lay a world of doubt and self-reproach.

You mustn't give way to doubt, Kuert told himself. The submarine's nationality didn't matter at present. All that mattered was here and now, this minute and the next.

The man beside the mast was so near he could hear him breathing. He lowered his voice to a whisper. 'Do you really think we'll make it, sir?' He'd been wanting to ask that question for days now.

'A few of us may, with luck. The Great Bear, keep it just abaft the starboard beam. Remember that.'

I will. Even if only a few of us make it, I'm going to be one of them.

Hours went by. He had relieved Schneidewind at the tiller and was sitting there, leaning on it. He could smell the emanations of his body, the foul stench issuing from his lips. Or was it fear he could smell? His neck was stiff, the arm resting on the tiller felt like a lifeless block of wood. His mouth was parched. He thought of the water in the shell-case beneath the stern seat.

A sip, just a sip. No one'll notice if I take a sip.

To sleep, if only for a second or two! To shut his eyes! It was becoming harder and harder to hold his head up. He gave a start: he'd dozed off for a moment. The tiller had escaped his grasp and the boat was heeling dangerously.

How do you hope to make it if you don't pull yourself together?

He brought them back on course, scooped up some sea-water in his palm and splashed the back of his neck, repeating the process whenever fatigue threatened to get the better of him.

The rain water in the shell-case had turned brown with rust overnight. Kuert passed it around as soon as it became light.

Jan Bahrend shook his head when the container reached him.

'Someone else can have my share,' he said. 'Give it to Stachnovski or the skipper, anyone.'

Weary though he was, Kuert sensed that something was wrong. Something in Bahrend's tone and manner gave him pause for thought. The ex-cook's shoulders seemed narrower, almost childlike. The life-jacket that had once fitted him snugly now hung loose.

'No arguments, Jan,' Kuert told him. 'Everyone bails, everyone gets his ration. Come on, drink up. Who knows when we'll get some more?'

Bahrend shook his head again. 'I don't want it, Fritz. I don't want any water and I don't want to do any more bailing either.' His gaunt face, with its frosting of grey stubble, became animated. He gave a mournful laugh. 'Why not drink it yourself? You can have my ration.' He eyed Kuert. 'You're still as fat as a pig. If anyone makes it, you will.'

His voice sank to a confidential whisper. 'We can't all survive, there are too damned many of us. Did you see Fujiyama when we sailed? Didn't I tell you what the Japs always say? I told you our number would be up in the end, didn't I? Didn't I tell you about Fujiyama?'

Kuert stood there with the shell-case in his hand. He didn't know what to do, he knew only that he had to do something to overcome the mumbled objections of this ageing man with the shoulders of a child.

He recalled the night of the sinking and the way Bahrend's hands had trembled when he begged a swallow of rum from

91

his canteen, recalled his own refusal to part with any. That was how it had been, wasn't it? He'd refused Jan a swig of rum, but why? He couldn't really remember. His mind was devoid of everything but a vague sense of guilt. He groped for something to say.

'What's the matter with you?' he said helplessly. 'You were going to stand us a slap-up dinner in Bordeaux, remember? Thirteen courses, you said.'

'Thirteen courses?' Bahrend gave an odd laugh. Then his face turned serious. 'I was a damned good cook. I lived for my cooking. I was proud of it, and you know what happens when you rob a man of his pride. Be honest, Fritz: was I really such a lousy cook?' He looked at Kuert anxiously, as if the answer to his question were vastly important to him.

'Who says you were a lousy cook? You were good. You were the best.' Kuert had a lump in his throat. 'Gaides always swore you were the finest cook in New York, and that's saying something, isn't it?'

'You bet it is. I don't know why I ever left there.'

'I wish I'd eaten at your place some time.'

'Well, too late now.'

Kuert tried to thrust the shell-case into Bahrend's hands, but he wouldn't take it. 'You have it,' he said. 'It's yours. You stand a chance. It'd be wasted on me.'

Shared out among the rest, Bahrend's ration provided another swallow apiece. Kuert felt drained of energy afterwards. He returned to his place in the stern and drowsed, intermittently aware of Bahrend leaning motionless against the mast.

All at once the boat heeled over. Startled, Kuert saw a tall figure poised on the gunwale. It was already too late to do anything.

Bahrend simply let himself fall overboard. He toppled into the sea slowly and stiffly, like a felled tree.

Water slopped over the gunwale. Even as Bahrend drifted astern, two men automatically began to bail it out.

Schneidewind had turned pale. His lips twitched. He stared at the dark hummock of Bahrend's rounded back, which the steep seas alternately revealed and hid from view, then at the sail. He looked from Kuert to the man in the water, then back at the sail. Finally he shook his head. 'Nothing to be done,' he said. 'We can't go about.'

Boywitt was praying.

Let him die, Kuert thought. *Be merciful, let him die quickly!*

Men kept afloat by life-jackets died no easy death. They might drift for a day, two days, until they summoned up the courage to let their heads loll below the surface, or until their efforts not to do so were terminated by exhaustion. If Bahrend had been seeking a quick, easy death, he couldn't have done worse.

Boywitt was still praying. The skipper sat there like a marble statue.

'Amen,' Boywitt murmured, and crossed himself.

Schneidewind said, 'We'd better be on our guard, Kuert. Things like that are catching. If there was a stampede the boat could capsize, and then we'd all be done for.'

Kuert was grateful for those words. At least the skipper's head was clear. He didn't want to think of Bahrend.

Don't look. Forget him, let him drown, let them all drown. We're too many for this cockleshell as it is. Only a few of us stand a chance, the skipper said so himself. Or was it Jan Bahrend? Who cares? The lighter the boat the better.

It took a while to bail out the water they'd shipped. Kuert had the impression that the dinghy was riding marginally higher in the water. A good thing, good for the rest of them.

Jan Bahrend? He had simply been a person who wasn't there any more. The only thing that scared him was the question of when it would be his turn.

The next morning brought storm-force winds and fifteen- to twenty-foot waves. Kuert cut his daily notch, the tenth.

He slept whenever he wasn't handling the sail, but sleeping and waking were almost indistinguishable now. Not even sleep had the power to confer oblivion. Even in his sleep he was aware of the dinghy's wild cavortings and Schneidewind's tense face as he grimly strove to prevent it from broaching to.

They capsized at about midday. Whether or not Schneidewind had dozed off at the helm, the boat overturned. The sail collapsed with a fluttering sound.

They were pitched into the sea like so many dolls. Kuert tried to catch hold of the grab-rope, but the waterlogged dinghy, which had sluggishly righted itself, was rotating on its axis like a piece of driftwood.

He could hear the others' cries. They were in the sea all around him, struggling to remain in the vicinity of the boat, squandering their strength by shouting and striking out wildly.

He saw Schaper, Hencke and Bergmann trying to scramble aboard the dinghy amidships. He was about to swim towards them and do likewise when his instinct for self-preservation deterred him. Knowing what would happen, he trod water and waited. The boat capsized once more, submerging the three men beneath it. Kuert continued to watch and wait, but they didn't reappear.

Looking round, he made out a white dot among dark waves. The skipper's cap! The sight smote him like an electric current. Anything but that, he thought. He swam towards the cap, only to find that Schneidewind was still wearing it.

'Tell them to distribute themselves fore and aft,' he gasped. 'We've got to hold her steady.'

Kuert passed the order on, shouting to make himself heard above the storm. He swam towards the boat, followed by Binder and Klockmann. 'Now!' They caught hold of the grab-rope.

'Who's up forward?' Kuert shouted. He could see three figures hanging on to the bow, but they were shrouded in spindrift.

'Stachnovski and Boywitt,' Binder said breathlessly, 'and the youngster, Waldemar.'

Three plus themselves and the Captain made seven. *Only seven now.*

Seven were missing, seven plus the dog. Kuert remembered

seeing the animal paddling wearily, confusedly, away from the boat.

The dinghy had steadied now that their weight was evenly distributed fore and aft. Only seven of them: Schneidewind, Binder, Klockmann, Stachnovski, Boywitt, Waldemar and himself. Were they the handful destined to survive?

'The rudder!'

The cry jolted Kuert out of his reverie. It was Schneidewind who had noticed that the rudder was gone.

It must have come unshipped when the boat capsized. My God, Kuert thought, what good was the dinghy without a rudder? And then the full truth dawned on him. The mast had also been carried away. So had the sail and the remains of the tarpaulin. The shell-case, too, was bound to have disappeared.

He didn't know how much time had elapsed, a few minutes or an hour, when he heard Schneidewind say, 'It's no use. We'll never get the water out of her.'

He stared at the boat, awash with sea water but denuded of everything else. The skipper was right. No rudder, no mast, no sail; what hope did they have? He was thinking quite clearly. Perhaps it was the chill of the sea that induced such lucidity. All that surprised him was his refusal to give up.

But another thought struck him too: *You were no better off the night the ship went down. All you had was an empty, water-logged boat.* He knew it wasn't so, knew that the situation had been quite different, there was no debris to salvage and he wasn't as strong now, but he also knew that he would keep going to the bitter end.

His decision to do so dated from some time in the past, he couldn't remember when. It had no connection with the *Doggerbank* or the other ships he'd sailed in, nor even with the war and his determination to survive it. It lay still further back. Perhaps it was a legacy from his miner father, who worked below ground and in constant danger. He had ruined his health down there, and for scant reward, but he was a stayer. Kuert knew that he himself could no more give up hope than take his own life.

The seven men clung to the grab-rope and drifted. It was all they could do. Hours went by, and the light began to fade. 'We won't last the night,' Schneidewind said. 'Not a hope.'

Kuert was in the water beside him. 'This storm can't last for ever. We'll get her shipshape again once it blows over.'

'We're in the tropics now,' Schneidewind said. 'In these latitudes, storms don't always blow over so quickly. No, we don't stand a chance.'

Catching sight of Binder's horrified face alongside, Kuert vaguely remembered what he had told them about the end of the life-raft. Fischer, the gun, the mania for self-destruction that had spread like a virulent disease, the eight shots.

Kuert looked at Schneidewind. He needed him. Schneidewind was his compass, his navigational aid. He could do without any of the others, but not Schneidewind.

'Klockmann,' he said, 'give me a hand with the skipper. Help me get him aboard.'

They gripped Schneidewind by the seat of his pants and boosted him over the gunwale. He didn't resist. Seated on the thwart thigh-deep in water and facing aft, he looked down at them.

'Listen to me,' he said. 'You must all decide for yourselves. As far as I'm concerned, it's over.'

Kuert, hanging on to the grab-rope, was looking straight up at him. Schneidewind's eyes, or what he could read in them, convinced him that the man was in deadly earnest.

He saw the skipper reach inside the neck of his sweater and feel for something. The gesture was yet another reminder of the moment when Binder had told them about the suicides on the life-raft. He hadn't attached any importance to it or grasped its significance at the time, but he did so now.

Schneidewind produced an oilskin pouch from under his sweater. The waterproof container was suspended from his neck by a thong, and the object inside it, clearly identifiable by it's shape, was an automatic pistol. He slipped the thong over his head and sat there with one hand holding the thwart and the other the pouch. His face, emaciated and thick with grey stubble, was as expressionless as his bloodshot, inflamed eyes. 'I'm going to make an end of myself while I still can.'

Kuert stared at the pouch. He couldn't let it happen. He must put up a fight for Schneidewind's survival; he needed him.

'At least wait till morning, skipper. The weather may improve.' He had to shout to make himself heard above the roar of the waves and the wind. 'Even if it doesn't, we'll bail her out somehow. At least wait till morning!'

Schneidewind shook his head. 'We haven't a hope.' The voice was unlike any voice Kuert had ever heard, the eyes stared straight through him. 'None of us will ever reach land.' He fingered the pouch. 'This is the best way out.'

No, Kuert told himself, *no, no, no!* He was incapable of any other thought. Schneidewind's resignation appalled him. The captain of the *Doggerbank* had always been so calm, so courageous and confident, a model of fortitude and endurance, a man who would never break, never give up. Was he right to give up now? *No, no, no!*

Kuert could not have said what gave him the strength to believe, even now, that he himself would survive. He had always known that his time would come some day, but he had buried that knowledge deep inside him and made it a rule never to let his thoughts stray beyond the immediate future.

Schneidewind had taken out the automatic. Kuert stared at it, struck by the contrast between the oily black metal and the pallor of the captain's skin. The gun was a threat to them all. For a moment he debated whether to knock it flying or push him off the thwart.

Then he felt Schneidewind's free hand on his shoulder.

'That wouldn't change anything, Kuert. Believe me, what's in store for us would be worse than this. It's easier to die now than. . .'

Kuert reasoned with him. He couldn't remember later what he said or what words he used. He begged and pleaded, simultaneously realizing that it was useless. Schneidewind's mind was made up, he knew, and the fact that nothing could change it robbed him of any further value.

The boat gave a sudden lurch. Stachnovski had swum aft and hitched one leg over the gunwale.

'Get off!' Kuert shouted. 'You'll capsize her!'

Stachnovski lowered himself into the water again. 'What's going on?' he demanded.

Kuert scanned his face. The parchment-like skin was drawn taut over the prominent cheekbones. It was the face of a stranger, a human wreck. His voice, too, sounded strange. He had spotted the gun in the skipper's hand and was staring at it fixedly.

'Get back where you were, Polack,' Kuert told him. 'I'll come with you.' He couldn't bear to look at the gun any longer. Even he might weaken in the end.

'What is it?' Stachnovski insisted. 'Is he planning to shoot himself?'

Schneidewind spoke before Kuert could reply. 'We're done for.'

'Just a minute!' Stachnovski yelled. He made an unsuccessful grab for the gun, lost his balance, and went under. Surfacing, he clung to the gunwale with both hands.

'You can't do that, skipper. Let us go first. We've just as much of a right to that gun as you. If you're going, take us with you!'

Let them, thought Kuert. *If they want to kill themselves, let them! I don't need anyone. I've got to get away from them, or they'll end by infecting me.*

Stachnovski argued with Schneidewind like a man possessed. 'This was our boat, skipper. We could have left you to die, but we didn't. This was our boat, ours! We didn't have to pick you up, so you owe us. If you're going to end it all, we will too.' There was no fear in Stachnovski's expression, just a mute plea to end his sufferings. 'Please. . .' The word issued from his cracked lips in an almost inaudible whisper. 'Go on, shoot me.'

Waldemar had swum aft too. He clung to the grab-rope, his body racked with sobs. 'Don't leave me behind,' he whimpered.

No one had been paying any attention to Binder, one of the four survivors from the life-raft.

'If I've got to die,' he said suddenly, 'I'd sooner drown.'

'You really think it's that easy?' Stachnovski muttered.

Binder didn't answer. He let go of the grab-rope and swam away from the boat. He swam powerfully, with a sudden, unaccountable burst of energy, and ploughed through the waves until he was out of sight.

'He's gone,' Stachnovski said in a bemused voice.

For a moment the others simply clung to the grab-rope, too shocked to move.

Schneidewind continued to gaze blankly into space. *Why don't I just give up?* Kuert asked himself, knowing all the time that he couldn't bring himself to do so.

Waldemar was still whimpering. Stachnovski had started pleading again, and Klockmann, too, was imploring Schneidewind to shoot him.

'Wait, all of you!' Kuert shouted. 'Let's wait till morning. Don't do it, Polack!'

But Stachnovski thrust him violently aside. He clung to the gunwale and shut his eyes, waiting. 'Please, Captain!'

Kuert saw Schneidewind take aim. He saw the gun's black muzzle barely a hand's breadth from Stachnovski's skull.

He turned away, overcome with horror, and swam for the bow. He was scared, afraid of weakening. It occurred to him that he might soon be alone. *Alone. Just me, the boat, and the sea.*

He could see Boywitt clinging to the bow of the dinghy. *He's the only one left*, Kuert thought. *Without him, I'd be all on my own!*

The first shot rang out before he could reach Boywitt, who had left his post and swum to meet him. Kuert pushed him back, propelled him towards the bow again.

'Don't be a fool, Papa, we'll make it. We'll get the boat going again, just the two of us. We'll make it, I promise you. Papa! Don't leave me!'

Boywitt was trembling all over. His lips moved in prayer: 'Thy kingdom come, Thy will be done.'

'Boywitt, Karl, Papa! Stop it! Please listen.' They heard a second shot, followed almost immediately by a third. 'Please, Papa! I promise you we'll make it!' He kept repeating the words like an incantation. The shots meant nothing, simply that the others weren't there any more. They were dead, but not even death was a reality. Boywitt was the only reality. His life depended on him now.

You'll never make it on your own!

'Let go of me,' Boywitt said. 'We're finished and you know it. If the skipper thinks so. . .'

The sail! Kuert thought. What was it about the sail? Something important, but what? *Jesus*, he prayed, *let me remember.*

'The sail's still there!' he said, surprised to hear himself speak with such conviction.

'The sail? How can it be?'

'Because we made it fast, Papa! Of course! We secured the mast and the sail to the boat, don't you remember?'

Boywitt shook his head. 'The skipper,' he said feebly, 'he'd never give up if we still stood a chance, not the skipper.'

'We'll make it, Papa! We'll make it, the two of us! Stay with me and I'll get you out of this.' *You've got to convince him, you've got to! You need him!* 'We've stuck it for ten days. Why give up now? It's pointless. Nobody would ever find out how we died. Your wife would never know. And what about your son, Papa? You told me about him, remember? Who's going to teach him to sail and fish?'

'Stop it, Fritz! For God's sake stop it!'

'I hear you praying all the time, but why bother, if you're planning to kill yourself? Since when does a good Catholic take his own life?'

'Stop it, please!' Boywitt's voice rose to a shout. 'All right, I'll stay, I promise I'll stay. I mean, if you really think we'll make it. Maybe you're right about the sail and the mast.'

A sudden sound transfixed them: Schneidewind was laughing to himself. It was Kuert who broke the spell. 'I'll have another word with him,' he said. 'It's worth a try. You stay here and hold the boat steady. You promised, don't forget.'

Alone now, Schneidewind was sitting on the thwart with the gun still in his hand.

The others weren't there any more, but the knowledge that they were dead left Kuert strangely unmoved. His horror had subsided.

'Boywitt's staying, skipper,' he said. 'We're going to try to make it.'

Schneidewind mightn't have heard him. There was a twisted smile on his face.

'Why not come with us, sir?'

'It's too late, I've had enough,' Schneidewind replied in a low, flat voice. 'Too many men have died. . . Too many – a whole crew. . .'

'We've still got the sail and the mast.' In Kuert's mind, this had now become an established fact.

Schneidewind looked down at him and shook his head. 'The Great Bear, Kuert.' His tone was suddenly matter-of-fact. 'Remember what I told you: the Great Bear, keep it just abaft the starboard beam.'

He put the pistol back in his pouch and cautiously, he waded aft to the stern seat. The rope that had been used to tow the raft was still secured to the transom. He wound the free end around his chest and knotted it. Kuert watched this procedure uncomprehendingly. *Boywitt's staying* was his only thought.

'This is the most I can do for you,' Schneidewind said. 'You can use me as a sea-anchor. It may help to keep the boat steady.'

He perched on the transom, took the pistol out of the pouch again, raised it and put it to his temple. Kuert could detect no trace of fear. He seemed the skipper they had always known: calm, collected, imperturbable.

Then he said, with total serenity, 'If you want the gun, you'd better look lively.'

They were his last words.

He squeezed the trigger. The report was followed by two splashes, the first as the automatic fell into the water-logged boat, the second as Schneidewind's body toppled over backwards into the sea. Kuert made no attempt to retrieve the gun. He had a terrible suspicion that the feel of the smooth, cold metal might prove too great a temptation.

He made his way back to the bow, half swimming, half-hauling himself along by the grab-rope.

Boywitt was praying again.

'We'll climb aboard,' Kuert said. 'You here, me in the stern. We'll try to bail her out, all right?'

Boywitt nodded mutely.

'Don't move till I say the word. Easy does it. If we capsize again, we're done for.'

He swam aft. The rope Schneidewind had knotted around his chest was slanting down into the water from the transom. It was taut, he noticed, but the sight aroused no particular emotion in him.

He signalled to Boywitt and climbed in over the stern, then waited until he saw the older man crouching in the bow.

'Easy, Papa! One step at a time!' They waded towards each other, keeping their centre of gravity low to avoid overturning the waterlogged boat.

They found the buoy-rope and hauled it in. When the mast and sail were floating alongside, they manhandled them cautiously over the gunwale.

'What did I tell you?' Kuert was too tired to feel triumphant. He felt for the knife rolled up in the waistband of his underpants and cut a square piece out of the sail. Then they started bailing.

They bailed for hours on end, taking it in turns, but to no effect. Any water they removed was quickly replaced by the waves that broke over the boat. It was the first time Kuert came close to giving up. Alone in the darkness with Boywitt, he began to feel that the skipper had been right after all, but he resisted the thought.

Boywitt didn't run out on you! You made him a promise. You can't give up now.

In the end they stopped bailing and lapsed into a kind of stupor, but even in this half-sleep they clung to the thwart

7. Fritz Kuert at the time of his transfer to the *Doggerbank*.

8. Members of the *Doggerbank's crew* photographed while on leave at the Japanese resort of Hakone in September, 1942.

9. *U43*, the German submarine that sank the *Doggerbank* off the Azores in 1943, believing it to be a British ship. Of the 365 German seamen on board, all but one perished.

10. The Italian freighter *Savoia* after being bombed off Brindisi in 1941. Boatswain Fritz Kuert survived four sinkings in vessels of this kind, which were employed as supply ships for the Afrika Korps.

11. Grand Admiral Dönitz, Commander-in-Chief U-boats, signed this photograph for Fritz Kuert, former boatswain of the *Doggerbank*, when the latter visited him in 1961.

12. Paul Schneidewind, Captain of the blockade-runner *Doggerbank*, formerly the British ship *Speybank*, was regarded as an exceptionally experienced skipper. It was his task to bring the *Doggerbank*, complete with her precious cargo of crude rubber and edible fats, safely through enemy-controlled waters from Japan to occupied France.

and each other. It was all that kept them from being washed overboard.

Roused by the coming of dawn, they sat up and surveyed the scene without a word. The sea was no calmer, the sky still heavily overcast. The night had been starless, Kuert remembered. He didn't think of the dead, only of the task that lay ahead. He began the day as he had begun all its predecessors, by cutting a notch in the gunwale, the eleventh. He gave Boywitt the little wedge of wood to chew. They bailed all day long. The dinghy was a little higher in the water by nightfall, but they could think themselves lucky it hadn't overturned.

The storm subsided during the night. The twelfth day, the twelfth notch. They started bailing again as soon as they awoke at dawn. This time they could definitely see the water-level sinking. The sight spurred them on, although they were both so weak that they flopped down exhausted every few minutes. They didn't succeed in ridding the dinghy of water entirely, but the bow and stern sheets were dry.

They set sail around midday. They reduced the mast to one oar and trimmed off part of the sail. Although the area of canvas exposed to the wind was smaller, the dinghy had previously held fifteen men. Now that there were only two of them, the reduced sail area was quite adequate.

The worst thing was the loss of the rudder, though the thing on the end of the tow-rope helped a little. To keep the boat on course they were obliged to make use of the oar no longer required for the mast, but holding it over the stern with one hand and guiding it with the other was such an effort that it sapped what little strength they had left.

Kuert's hands would seize up after steering with the oar for fifteen minutes. He shivered with cold and fatigue, the mast danced before his eyes, his body felt like a cold, empty shell.

At moments like these he hovered on the brink of final defeat. His mainstay, curiously enough, was the thought of Boywitt, the determination to get him safe home to his wife and son. It tapped a store of energy he hadn't known he possessed. It was his defence against everything, the pain that racked his body and the doubts that tormented his mind.

Darkness fell, but no stars could be seen. Dawn broke, and there was nothing in sight but sea and sky.

Kuert no longer had the strength to hold the steering-oar. To avoid capsizing, they had to lower the sail.

Boywitt, huddled in the bow, kept moaning and begging for water. Kuert tried not to hear him. The old fisherman's face was a single, agonized entreaty. His appeals for water were gradually eroding Kuert's strength, his will to survive. Something had to be done, he knew.

It was then, on the morning of the thirteenth day, that he first saw the sharks. He spotted them keeping pace with the dinghy only fifteen or twenty feet astern. Boywitt must have noticed them too, because he suddenly fell silent. Kuert could see their dorsal fins jutting from the water, thin and sharp as scythes. He counted two big fish and four smaller ones.

Uneasily, he watched them following the boat. Blood, he thought vaguely, they're drawn to the scent of blood. His eyes fell on the tow-rope slanting down into the water. So that was what had attracted them!

The best policy would have been simply to cut the rope and let the corpse fall astern, taking the sharks with it, but Kuert was reluctant to sacrifice a few feet of rope. One never knew when it might come in useful.

His hands were raw, but he grasped the rope and hauled it in. It surprised him how easily it came, until he saw what was on the end. Schneidewind's corpse had been horribly diminished. The arms and legs were gone; only the head and trunk remained attached to the rope. The sharks. Kuert went numb with horror at the thought that they had been there during the night, unseen but only a few feet away.

He let the mangled remains flop back into the water and cut the rope. *That's six or seven feet of rope I've lost*, he thought. Although the mutilated corpse meant less to him than the loss of the rope, he suddenly wished he'd died with the others. To him, death had become synonymous with an end to pain. He could understand Schneidewind now. How easy it was to put a bullet in your head. On the other hand, what was the point of all his sufferings if he failed the final test?

Schneidewind had said nothing about sharks, or had the thought occurred to him? No sign of them now. *But they'll show up again. They never tire, never give up. All they have to do is follow us. They're in no hurry. They know they'll get us in the end.*

It did him good to hate them. Hatred galvanized him, gave him renewed strength. It was good to know that the boat was their only protection. *Or our coffin.*

He pictured the way it would be: two corpses drifting ever further across the ocean until they were washed up on some foreign shore. He pictured a group of figures clustered around their floating coffin, staring down at its two nameless occupants.

He stared at the rope in his hands. *Do something!* he commanded himself. *For Boywitt's sake, for your own. For Schneidewind, Bahrend, Stachnovski, young Waldemar. Do something!*

He crawled to the bow. Boywitt gave him an imploring look.

'Water, Fritz! Just a mouthful!'

Kuert took out the pocket-knife. 'We're going to make ourselves a rudder, Papa.'

'A rudder?' Boywitt stared at him incredulously. 'How?'

'We'll do it, Papa. We're going to make ourselves a rudder, and we're going to make it home.'

He began by cutting the forward thwart in half. Bisecting the inch-thick plank was relatively easy. He scored it with the knife. Then, working slowly and carefully to avoid snapping the blade, he progressively deepened the incision until the thwart broke under his weight.

The hardest part was extracting the two nails at either end of the thwart. First he exposed the heads by chipping away the wood around them bit by bit. The nails remained firmly embedded. He wrenched at them until the blood seeped from

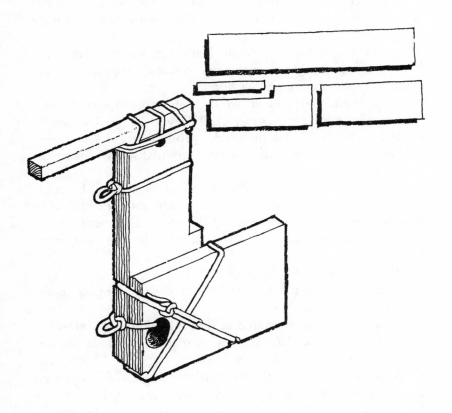

under his fingernails. He licked off the blood and tried using his teeth instead.

It took him several hours to extract one pair of nails. The other two were easier to get out using the board as a lever, but he had to be careful: all four nails were essential to what he had in mind.

By the time the light began to fade, the fruits of his day's labours were as follows: the two halves of the forward thwart; four two-and-a-half-inch nails; a length of rope; and a makeshift tiller cut from the thwart that held the mast.

He was exhausted, so much so that he feared he might collapse at any moment. There were times when he drifted into unconsciousness, but he worked on long after nightfall, not stopping until he had assembled all his components. The rudder was finished at last.

Next morning he cut the fourteenth notch. Then, with Boywitt's help, he secured the rudder to the gudgeons with rope. He felt proud of himself. And of Boywitt. And of the fact that they made such a good team. His hands were bleeding and covered with suppurating sores. He sluiced them with sea water.

They'll heal, he told himself. *The less you think about them, the sooner they'll heal. All you've got to do is keep your wits about you and sail, sail like the skipper said. You're the skipper now!*

The weather had improved. The sun was shining, but he felt no warmer. He was made up of separate, discrete parts, all of them agonizingly painful: torn hands, oozing sores, throat swollen with thirst, eyes smarting and half blinded.

The days went by in a dreamlike succession. The nights were merely dreams of a different, more horrific kind.

Now that they had a rudder they could sail again, but half an hour at the tiller was enough to drain him of energy. He would simply stretch out in the bottom of the boat, and Boywitt would crawl aft and take over. Then came his turn again, then Boywitt's. No words were exchanged on these occasions. To speak, to move their cracked, raw lips, would have been too great an effort. For all that, it was good not to be alone. Even though they rarely spoke, being alone would have meant surrender and death.

Boywitt had stopped begging for water, not aloud at any rate, but his eyes craved it incessantly.

The fine, sunny weather persisted, the trade wind blew steadily. The sharks had resumed their shadowy pursuit. There were two or three big adults. The others were younger and smaller.

Toward noon on the fifteenth day, while Kuert was asleep, Boywitt lowered the sail because the wind had become too strong. When they came to raise it again they almost failed. Even their concerted efforts were barely sufficient to set it. They would have to risk leaving it up; they had no choice.

On the night of the seventeenth day Boywitt heard, or claimed to have heard, the sound of a ship's propellers.

Kuert didn't believe in Boywitt's ship, neither that one nor the next. All he believed in was the wind. The wind was their ally. And so, with senses dulled and minds emptied of all but the most rudimentary thoughts, they sailed on as the wind, sun and stars dictated.

Getting Boywitt home: for Kuert, that was the only thing that still possessed any reality.

On the eighteenth day Boywitt failed to relieve Kuert at the helm. Although it was his turn, he lay in the bow without stirring. Kuert lashed the tiller and crawled over to him. To stand up and walk was out of the question; he crawled on his hands and knees.

'Time to take over, Papa.' Every word was a supreme effort.

Boywitt gave a start and struggled into a sitting position. 'I don't have the strength, Fritz. I'm through. Give me a drink, give me some water, please.' He was weeping dry-eyed.

The sight of him wrung Kuert's heart. His face was nothing but skin and bone and sores. The blue seaman's jacket, bleached grey by sea water, hung loose. Kuert could smell the stench given off by his clothes, which were rotting on his body. He sat there, a pitiful, stinking human wreck.

Is that how I look, too?

'You've got to relieve me, Papa. I can't go on.'

'I'll relieve you, but give me something to drink. Please, just a sip.'

His plea left Kuert unmoved. It merely intensified his own agonies of thirst.

'Why won't you let me drink some sea water, Fritz? A mouthful wouldn't hurt, surely?'

This time Kuert was alarmed. He tried to raise his voice. 'Stop that! Sea water's out!'

'Go on, just a mouthful. It won't do me any harm, and I'll stand your watch all day long.'

'It'll kill you, Papa. Sea water will do for you.' He couldn't remember why this was so. They'd discussed the subject in the days immediately after the sinking, when they were all together in the boat. Schneidewind had warned them time and again not to drink any sea water. He'd spoken of seeing shipwrecked sailors who had done so and defied all medical attempts to save them. Kuert had forgotten the precise reason. All he knew was, it was a temptation to resist at all costs.

'It'll kill you,' he repeated. 'Be reasonable, Papa. I don't have any water.'

But Boywitt wouldn't be silenced. His pleas sent Kuert wild with thirst. He couldn't bear to hear them any longer. Leaving him huddled in the bow, he crawled back to the tiller.

That afternoon Boywitt started singing. Kuert was amazed at the sudden steadiness and clarity of the old fisherman's voice. He sang hymns, most of them unfamiliar to Kuert.

Boywitt continued to sing all afternoon, pausing only when exhaustion got the better of him. The words eventually became unintelligible, though Kuert could sometimes recognize the melodies. Then even the melodies degenerated into a monotonous singsong interspersed with ever-lengthening pauses.

The singing didn't trouble Kuert at first, but in the end,

afraid that Boywitt was cracking up, he couldn't stand it any longer.

He crawled back to the bow. 'Come with me, Papa.' He put an arm round Boywitt's shoulders and hauled him aft. It was only now, with the other man close beside him, that he realized how scared he was of solitude.

'I'm sorry, Fritz,' Boywitt muttered, 'I'm just a burden to you. Leave me be.' A little while later he even offered to take the helm.

Kuert shook his head. He couldn't have slept in any case. Even if he relinquished the tiller to Boywitt he would still have to keep an eye on him, so it made no difference.

All the same, it was good to have someone at his side, however useless.

I've got to pull him through, he kept telling himself. He began talking to Boywitt. What did he know about his background?

There was his boat, for a start: it had a red sail, Boywitt had confided. That sail was known all along the coast. Everyone who saw it knew that it belonged to Karl Boywitt, the trawlerman.

So Kuert talked about the boat with the red sail, that and anything else that came into his head. Boywitt grew calmer, so he talked on. It never struck him that his words were barely coherent, and that they, too, had degenerated into a monotonous singsong.

When he emerged from his torpor the next morning Boywitt was beside him no longer.

He's gone and left me, he thought bitterly.

But no, Boywitt had resumed his place in the bow during the night and was lying there with his face pillowed on his arms.

He wasn't asleep, though. When Kuert crawled over to him he slowly sat up. His expression had changed to one of almost preternatural serenity. Kuert stared at the face that was, yet was not, Karl Boywitt's. Then he caught a whiff of his breath and knew at once what had happened. The stench from their empty bellies was frightful. Kuert had grown used to it long ago, but today Boywitt's breath assailed his nostrils like the miasma from a plague pit. And then he saw his mouth. It was open. The lips were grey, and white crystals were adhering to the corners of the mouth and the grizzled beard. Kuert stared at the salt that had accumulated there.

'What have you been up to, Papa?' He waited for an answer, although he knew it already. He gripped Boywitt by the shoulders and shook him. 'You've been drinking sea water!'

Very feebly, as if they weren't talking about him at all, Boywitt shook his head. 'Leave me be, Fritz.'

'It'll kill you, Papa! I told you it would!' Kuert began to weep with anger at Boywitt's stupidity, with despair at having failed to preserve him from it. *Why didn't you take better care of him?*

But another thought took shape at the back of his mind: *You'll have to make the best of it.*

'I couldn't take it any more, Fritz.'

Kuert let go of him, unable to endure their physical contact a moment longer. It was like the time when Schneidewind's gun fell into the boat and he hadn't trusted himself to resist the feel of it.

He left Boywitt and crawled back to the tiller. The other thought was steadily becoming clearer and more distinct: *He's been drinking sea water. He won't be with you much longer. You'll have to manage without him.*

Something inside him rebelled at the idea, but he knew at the same time that his only surviving companion was doomed. *You must write him off.* He glanced at Boywitt from time to time, vainly awaiting some reaction.

That afternoon Boywitt started to sing again in a hoarse, sobbing voice. During the night, while Kuert was asleep, he drank some more sea water. Kuert, who could tell this was so when morning came, knew that he would soon be alone.

He added a notch to the others in the gunwale and tried to count them, but they swam before his eyes. He ran his finger along them like a blind man: nineteen. *Nineteen days.*

The sunlight, though harsh and glaring, was devoid of warmth. The wind had dropped, the sail hung limp. There

111

was nothing to be seen on either quarter but an expanse of unruffled, deep blue sea, a great silence through which the boat slowly drifted. Seated in the stern, he glided on through that profound, illimitable silence.

Keep going, he told himself. *If you ever want to see land again, keep going.* He had to use every bit of strength left in him, because now he was the only survivor of the *Doggerbank*.

The rain came on the twenty-first day. The sky had become overcast the day before. Kuert watched the dark, brooding clouds with tense expectancy. Boywitt had been lying slumped in the bow for two whole days and nights. At first Kuert had heard him praying softly, plaintively, but he had been silent for for a long time now.

Was he dead? Was he still alive? Kuert had left him undisturbed. The eighteen feet from the stern sheets to the bow were too much for him. He needed all his remaining strength to sail the boat.

He felt no elation even when, at noon on that twenty-first day, the heavens finally opened. He sat there in the gently falling rain, a prey to indecision. If he wanted to drink he would have to lower the sail, but he was afraid to do so.

At length he crawled forward, lowered the sail and spread it out to catch the rain.

Boywitt still didn't move, but Boywitt was the least of Kuert's concerns as he rinsed the salt off the canvas and spread it out again. His raging thirst preoccupied him to the exclusion of all else. Not a morsel of food had passed his lips for twenty-one days, and it was twelve since his last few mouthfuls of rusty water.

The rain was terribly slow to accumulate in the canvas trough. Kuert lapped it up greedily as soon as an inch or two had collected. The water ran down his chin and chest. He must have drunk at least a bucketful before it occurred to him that Boywitt hadn't moved.

He hauled himself to his feet by the mast and clung to it. 'Papa!' he called. 'Come on, it's raining!'

The old fisherman still didn't stir. He was lying in the bow with his face upturned, eyes shut and mouth open. He might have been asleep.

'Here, Papa! Now you can drink as much as you like.'

He climbed unsteadily over the thwart.

He saw the rain on Boywitt's face. It was trickling down his forehead and his hollow, bearded cheeks, trickling into the sunken eyes and the open mouth that resembled a hole in the middle of a parched field.

Kuert knelt down beside him, bent over him. He felt as if someone had stabbed him and twisted the knife in the wound. Boywitt's cracked and bloated lips were quince-yellow. Pus was seeping from the corner of his mouth.

Kuert gave a shudder and briefly averted his eyes. 'Why couldn't you have waited, Papa? Why did you have to drink that stuff? I told you it would kill you. Now it's raining. Come on.'

The rain was heavier now. He could hear it pattering on the outspread sail. When he turned to look, it was full to the brim.

'Look, Papa! All that lovely water!'

He bent lower and stared into Boywitt's face, still hoping against hope that he might be asleep.

'I can't drink it all on my own. Here, I'll help you.'

Boywitt made no sound as Kuert put a hand beneath his back and raised him a little. His head lolled sideways, his arms hung limp. Kuert knew he was dead, but he still refused to accept the fact.

He crawled back to the sail and drank some more, half-expecting Boywitt to sit up at any moment and join him.

At least I've got enough water to last me now.

It took a while to dawn on him that he had no way of storing the water, no receptacle of any kind. If he wanted to sail on, he would have to do without it.

It's one or the other: drink or sail.

The rain had stopped. He stared at the brimming tarpaulin. It was an inconceivable thought, jettisoning all that water, the glorious water for which he'd waited so long. Helplessly, he looked at Boywitt.

'Tell me what to do, Papa.'

He would be done for if he didn't sail on. But what if it were pointless to keep sailing? What if he never reached land at all? Mightn't it be better to retain the water and hold out for a few more days on the off-chance that some ship might pick him up?

'What should I do, Papa, tell me! What should I do?'

It was an inhuman decision that confronted him. It seemed harder than any he had ever been called upon to make, and he had to make it alone.

He sobbed silently, feebly, as he wrestled with the problem. He stripped off his ragged clothes, scooped up some water in his palm and emptied it over himself. Cuts and abrasions covered his entire body like leprosy. Every little scratch was festering from exposure to sea water. The skin was broken in innumerable places. There were deep, suppurating sores on his hands and his knees. He sluiced his wounds, conscious all the time that he was only postponing an inescapable decision.

You've got to keep going. But he dreaded the exertion. Raising the sail by himself, without Boywitt's assistance, seemed an impossibility; they had only just managed it between them, and that was many days ago. What if he emptied the rain-water into the boat? There were a few inches of sea water amidships. Perhaps it would be drinkable if he diluted it. Lifting a corner of the sail, he emptied its contents into the bottom of the boat.

He grasped the rope in his raw hands, but the weight of the sail proved too much for him. He was at the end of his tether, on the point of giving up. He had shed no tears for Boywitt, but now they were streaming down his cheeks. He wasn't aware of them, only of the physical weakness that prevented him from raising the sail. *You can't give up now.*

He climbed on the thwart in which the mast was stepped, tied the rope around his chest, and let himself go limp. The rope cut into his ribs, lacerating the skin, but the weight of his body raised the sail a couple of feet. *You'll make it.*

Hand over hand he hauled himself erect, re-secured the rope around his chest, and went limp again: another couple of feet.

He had to repeat the process five times before the sail was set.

Afterwards, back in the stern sheets and thirsty again already, he eyed the water at his feet. He thought of Boywitt and his salt-seared throat. He was scared, uncertain how much longer he would be able to resist the temptation to drink the water in the bilge. He would persuade himself that it wouldn't harm him. In the end, if there were any left, he would drink it.

He secured the tiller and crawled forward. Taking the little square of canvas they had used as a bailer when the boat capsized, he emptied the bilge rather than surrender to the urge to drink it later on.

He sailed on with the dead man still aboard. He cut his notches in the gunwale, slowly chewed the fragments of wood, and sailed on. The days and nights seemed almost indistinguishable. He never left the stern seat now. He would doze off, be jolted awake by some untoward movement of the boat or the sail, and return to the present for another spell. His mind still rejected the fact of Boywitt's death. Was he really dead? Whatever the truth, he was grateful for the continued presence of the figure in the bow. He could look at it and feel that he wasn't alone. Sometimes he strained his ears as if expecting to hear it plead for water.

But he was soon compelled to accept the truth. The sun had been beating down on the boat ever since the day the heavens opened, and the stench from the bow was becoming more and more intolerable. He long resisted the thought of consigning Boywitt to the sea. It seemed a form of betrayal. Besides, there were the sharks. They had never ceased to shadow the boat.

On the twenty-third day the stench became so bad that it forced his hand. He waited until dusk, Boywitt's favourite time of day, the time when the first stars appeared and he would sit, silently communing with them, on top of the *Doggerbank*'s monkey island.

'I've no choice, Papa.' Kuert found it quite natural to speak the words aloud. 'I wanted you to be there when we sight land, but I don't have any choice. Please forgive me.'

He looked at the sharks, Boywitt's grave-diggers. Taking hold of his legs, he heaved them across the gunwale and rolled the rest of him overboard. He watched the motionless body drift away. The sharks darted forward at once, snapping at its extremities.

Take a look! Take a good look, then you'll know what you're in for if the boat overturns. If you've got to die, die on board.

Not for the first time, his eyes strayed to something in the bottom of the boat: Schneidewind's automatic was lying in the stern sheets, exactly where it had fallen from the skipper's hand so many days ago. Kuert had never dared to touch the gun. Sea water had penetrated its film of oil and patches of rust had formed on the bluish steel. Was there a round left in the chamber? Would the trigger mechanism work? If the answer to both these questions was yes, he had a ready means of ensuring that the sharks never devoured him alive. He banished the thought from his mind with a conscious effort, but he couldn't bring himself, even now, to pick up the gun and toss it overboard in case his resolution weakened.

Still fighting over Boywitt's meagre remains, the big fish fell astern. Kuert watched them across the widening expanse of water. He felt very alone.

It had become a habit, suffering from thirst, enduring pain and fear. He possessed neither pride nor a will of his own, merely the knowledge that in the boat he was safe from sharks.

The worst of it was, nothing happened. He was alone, utterly alone. That was all. Even the wind deserted him. By day the sea was like glass, the sail hung limp as a shroud. At night a gentle breeze would spring up, so that was when he made progress. He was still on course. He kept the Great Bear just abaft the starboard beam, as the skipper had instructed him. During the day, when the wind dropped, he simply drifted. The sharks were still following.

Toward noon on the day he cut the twenty-fourth notch,

the sharks startled a shoal of flying fish, one of which collided with the sail. It skimmed through the air on its gossamer fins, hit the canvas, and dropped into the bottom of the boat.

He pounced on the wriggling, flapping creature, which was no bigger than a herring, and twisted its head off. He sucked the blood that oozed from the gills. He didn't feel hungry, but he commanded himself to eat; he needed energy. Flying fish were a delicacy, he remembered Bahrend saying. He bit a chunk of flesh off the backbone. It was soggy and tasteless.

He chewed the mouthful and tried to swallow it, but his throat was too constricted. He spat out the skin and put the remainder of the fish on the thwart to dry. The heat intensified his thirst. The sun was blisteringly hot. Almost directly overhead, it beat down upon him without mercy.

He had only to turn his head to feel as if he were spiralling down into an abyss. Unable to sit upright any longer, he lashed the tiller and subsided into the bottom of the boat.

The sunlight's reflected glare was unendurable. Sweat ran into his eyes like molten lead. He seemed to see everything through a film of salt. His face was so dry he could feel the skin drawn tight over his cheekbones. His raw throat was on fire.

That afternoon he couldn't stand it any more. He crawled to the mast on all fours. He knew he would never manage to raise the sail again, but he didn't care, he had to have some protection from the sun. Everything swam before his eyes as he released the rope.

He hated his weakness, his thirst, his cuts and sores, but he lectured himself even now.

You'll make it. You still believe you'll make it. You'll never give up.

He was no longer aware of what he was doing. He only knew he wanted to find out which of them would prevail, his weakened body or his unbroken spirit.

He draped the sail over the bow, crawled into its shade, and stretched out on the spot where Boywitt had died. The slight upward sweep of the bow created a sort of couch, the most comfortable place in the entire boat.

It was wonderful just to lie there after so many days at the tiller, just to lie there with the sail overhead, dozing lethargically.

The twenty-fifth day dawned, and still he lay drowsing beneath the sail. Sometimes he watched the sharks swimming alongside. He could make out their steel-blue backs just below the surface. Sometimes he was awakened by a faint vibration as they dived beneath the boat. He had lost all fear of them. On the contrary, he was happy to have them there, occupying his thoughts. They were now his sole companions.

There were more sharks than there had been before. It almost made him feel guilty to lie watching them instead of sitting at the tiller. They escorted the boat on either side. What superb swimmers they were, even the young ones, tireless and tenacious!

He had heard of boats being overturned by sharks, but he felt sure these creatures meant him no harm when they made for the cool depths beneath the hull. Like him, they were merely seeking shade.

He would be roused, time and again, by the sound of their tails lashing the water before they dived. He would feel a tremor run through the hull beneath him, turn his head, and see them break surface on the other side, their sleek bodies momentarily burnished silver by the sunlight.

Welcome though the sharks were, he yearned for another human being to talk to. All he had left were memories, and they were poor company.

One of his recurrent mental images was of the fountain in the middle of the school playground, a grey cinder yard. Beside it hung a tin mug on a chain, but the boys never used it. They bent over the rim of the basin and held their mouths to the water as it left the iron spout. The school fountain figured prominently among his recollections. He saw the water gushing from the pipe in a thick stream, but the fountain was permanently besieged by other boys. He was always the last in line. Eventually he thrust them aside. He heard the splash of the water, saw it gushing from the pipe, bent over the edge of the basin, cupped his hands. Then he gave a start: a shark had lashed the sea with its tail.

His mother hated sharks, he recalled. He had returned from a trip to Venezuela with some dried shark fins as a souvenir. He could still hear her exclamation of disgust, see her upraised hands. 'I'm not having those in the house, my boy!'

The house. The countless houses like it, all identical, all begrimed with coal dust from the Gneisenau Pit. The little collier's cottage, the narrow passage where he slept when at home because there was no room for him anywhere else.

He wondered how his mother would greet the news of his death. He saw the postman lean his bicycle against the grimy wall and ring the bell.

She would take the letter and go to the living-room, put it on the sideboard. She wouldn't open it. She'd wait until his father came home from the pit.

But it wasn't time yet. She would put the envelope in the midst of the family photographs and the souvenirs he'd brought back from his voyages, propped against the sailing ship in the whisky bottle.

He saw the leather sofa beside the stove, the dip at one end, his father's favourite place. That was where he would open the letter, nails black with coal dust, while his wife sat stiffly on one of the hard, uncomfortable chairs at the round table.

How would the letter be worded?

All at once he saw other letters and other postmen pedalling to various destinations. Schneidewind, Waldemar Ring, Binder, Bahrend, Boywitt . . .

He saw their womenfolk take the letters, and all of them had his mother's face.

His memories of the dead were as vivid as if they had all been his brothers.

You mustn't give up, not now. They can't have died for nothing.

He no longer knew what day it was. He had cut another notch that morning, the twenty-sixth, not that he was capable of counting. His strength was almost gone, and he knew it.

119

One day they would find him, a nameless corpse adrift in a nameless boat.

Still holding the knife, he rolled over on his side. His bones seemed close to snapping every time he moved.

Slowly and painfully, letter by letter, he carved some words into the wood: name, nationality, place of birth, last ship.

You've got your coffin now, a big one all to yourself, complete with your name on it.

It was all over.

Nothing more to do but wait, wait and see what it's like to die.

That was when he saw the bird. It was hovering high overhead, immensely high, with dark, outspread wings. Was he only imagining it, or did the bird have some connection with death?

He could hardly breathe. He lay on his back and stared up at the sky. The bird had begun to gyrate. It described one sweeping circle, then another, then hovered once more on dark, motionless wings.

He stared at it transfixed, conscious of the pulse throbbing in his throat. The sight of the bird tormented him. It meant something unintelligible to him, something momentous, but its significance eluded him. It was like a long-awaited message that had proved to be undecipherable.

The bird resumed its gyrations, steadily receding until he could see it no more.

It was a bird! You aren't going mad. It looked like a hawk, only bigger and darker.

He gave a start of fear. Had Boywitt, too, seen the bird before death claimed him?

The sun was at its zenith. Its light showered down on him like incandescent rain. He crawled back under the sail.

Only the sharks were there now.

The sharks? No shark would produce that peculiar pounding in his ears. Perhaps it was another harbinger of death, like the big, black bird.

The strange sound grew louder, its rhythmical churning more distinct. He could think of only one thing that made such a sound: the propellers of a ship in ballast.

And he remembered that Boywitt had spoken of hearing a ship's propellers before he died.

PART THREE

THE SURVIVOR

The second officer of the *Campoamor* had come on watch at noon. A tanker sailing under the neutral flag of Spain, the *Campoamor* was owned by CAMPSA, the national petroleum monopoly. The 10,000 ton ship had left Barcelona two weeks before, on 15 March, 1943, with orders to pick up a cargo of Venezuelan petroleum. She was due to reach her destination, the island of Aruba in the Netherlands Antilles, in two days' time.

The day was very hot and almost windless. A dozen sharks were gambolling in the distance. The second officer watched them for a while from the wing of the bridge. The sight of so many sharks so far out to sea puzzled him. At length he turned to the messenger and told him to fetch the Captain.

When Joaquin Diaz appeared on the bridge, the second officer indicated a spot off the port bow. 'Sharks, sir, a lot of them, and all sticking close together. Looks odd. What do you make of it?'

Captain Diaz borrowed his binoculars and trained them on the sharks, which caught the sunlight whenever they broke surface. It was certainly unusual to see so many so far from land, but where was their prospective prey? There were no other vessels in sight.

Diaz continued to watch the sharks as they flashed and scintillated in the sunlight. And then, quite suddenly, he spotted the boat, a dinghy. But for the sharks, the two men realized later, they would never have noticed it.

Through the binoculars, Diaz made out a stumpy mast stepped amidships. There was no sail, just a tarpaulin draped over the bow, and no sign of anyone on board. The dinghy's bow bore no discernible name.

'Derelict, from the look of it.' Diaz lowered the binoculars. The dinghy was too small to be a fishing boat, and besides, no one would have ventured so far out to sea in such a craft.

The *Campoamor*'s course had brought her closer to the boat, which now lay almost abeam and was visible with the naked eye. It drifted slowly nearer, still escorted by its attendant sharks.

The second officer looked at Diaz inquiringly. The captain hesitated. He could ill afford to lose any time. It had been a long voyage by way of their prescribed route across the Atlantic, a special shipping lane reserved for neutral vessels, and he was hoping to pass Martinique and enter the Caribbean at daybreak. On the other hand, the sharks' tenacity suggested that the boat contained human prey of some kind.

It was the sharks that finally persuaded him. 'Stop engines,' he ordered, 'and send Carducho to me.'

The *Campoamor*'s boatswain was a giant of a man. 'I'm going to try to manoeuvre in close,' Diaz told him. 'Get down there and take a look. You know the form, Carducho: no clothing, no bits and pieces, nothing but the man himself, if there is one. Don't touch more than you have to. I don't want any disease on board.'

The following entry appears in the *Campoamor*'s log:

Stopped engines at 13.32 to examine a boat adrift at 15° 31' north, 51° west.

The date was 29 March, 1943, a Thursday. It was twenty-six days since the sinking of the *Doggerbank*. When sighted by the Spanish tanker, the dinghy was 1600 nautical miles from the spot where the ship had gone down.

The strange sound had stopped. Even the sunlight, which had rendered the canvas above his head translucent, was blotted out. Kuert lay there in the sudden gloom, at a loss to understand what had happened. He tried to sit up, but he was too weak, so he raised his hand and pushed the sail aside. The big, dark shape was right alongside. It towered over him like the side of a ship.

So you still believe in miracles, even now, he thought vaguely. He peered at the dark wall looming above him. *Rivets, portholes*. The dinghy was bumping against *metal*.

That bird, it had looked like a hawk. That was it! A hawk, a land bird, so land couldn't be that far off. The churning noise had sounded like a ship's propellers and the dark shape resembled a ship's side. And that thing up there? Red-yellow-red: a Spanish flag? He tried to shout, but all that

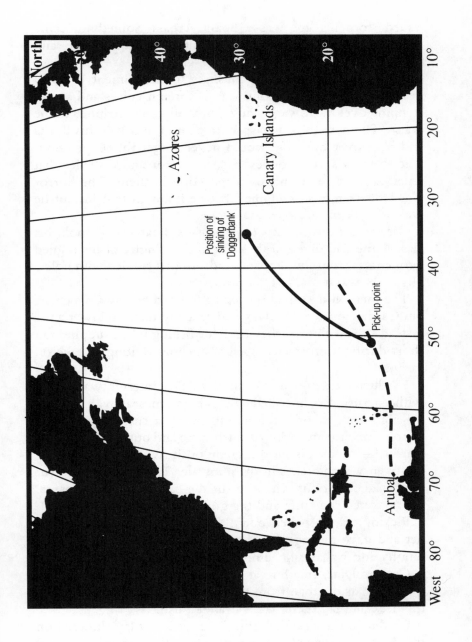

issued from his lips was a hoarse croak. Something came tumbling down the dark wall, swung from side to side, and finally steadied: a Jacob's ladder.

He must have lost consciousness for a moment or two, because his next recollection was of foreign voices and a man stepping over the thwart; a huge, muscular man stripped to the waist. The man took a clasp-knife from the belt of his ducks and bent over him. He would never forget that expression. The stranger's eyes conveyed such horror and disbelief that Kuert seemed to see his own reflection in them. The horror was so extreme, so genuine, that he knew in that instant he was safe. Then he passed out again.

Diego Carducho, the *Campoamor*'s boatswain, took his clasp-knife and divested the man in the dinghy of his ragged garments, a pair of underpants and a singlet riddled with holes. His body was a mass of cuts and sores.

The men on deck had started to lower a boatswain's chair, but Carducho waved it away and called to them to lower a net instead. It was the one they used for fishing when supplies ran short during a protracted spell at anchor, waiting to take on cargo.

Carducho examined the dinghy. The interior was white with encrusted, sun-baked salt. The stern seat was stained, possibly with blood, and beneath it lay a rusting automatic pistol. The dried remains of a fish were laid out on the thwart. Carducho shook his head incredulously when he discovered the twenty-six notches in the gunwale. The knife used to cut them had fallen out when he slit the castaway's underpants. He pocketed the knife and the gun.

Picking up the naked body, Carducho deposited it in the net and gave the signal to hoist away. Then, having set the dinghy adrift again, he climbed back up the ladder.

Captain Diaz, standing at the rail with several of his crew, looked on as the man from the dinghy was gently lowered to the deck and lay there like a stranded fish.

Carducho disentangled him. The castaway lay slumped on the deck, a human skeleton with a month's growth of beard and a body covered in suppurating sores. The men of the *Campoamor* recoiled at the sight of him. One by one they raised their hands and made the sign of the cross. Carducho picked up the man's limp form – he was easy enough to lift – and carried him below to the sick bay.

Afterwards, back on the bridge, Captain Diaz watched the dinghy fall slowly astern. The sharks had disappeared.

The castaway was still unconscious when Diaz called the sick bay a little while later. He went to the desk on which the *Campoamor's* log lay open and wrote:

At 13.40 we hove to beside the dinghy and found it to contain a castaway in the last stages of exhaustion. We picked him up and proceeded on our way. The said castaway is currently unable to make a statement because of his physical and mental condition. He is receiving first aid.

U43 was returning to base after three months on patrol in the Atlantic. On the morning of 31 March, 1943, two days after Kuert was picked up, the French coast near Lorient loomed out of the morning mist. It promised to be a fine, sunny day. Barrage-breakers had already taken *U43* under their wing and were guiding it through the minefields that screened the big U-boat base.

Oberleutnant Hans-Joachim Schwantke, *U43's* skipper, was standing beneath the single pennant flying from the half-extended periscope – one only, signifying only one ship sunk. Unlike the rest of the U-boat group to which he had been assigned, whose convoy operation had ended in failure, he had been lucky to sink at least one ship, a British vessel of almost 10,000 tons, his very first kill.

Schwantke could now see the jagged skyline of Lorient itself, which had been devastated by Allied air raids. Before long the U-boat base came into view, a series of ugly, flat-topped bunkers with featureless concrete walls.

He was glad when *U43* finally glided into its shadowy pen. For the first time in three months, he could feel safe from enemy bombs and depth-charges.

Schwantke was in absolutely no doubt at this stage that the unescorted ship he had sunk was British. Like all U-boat commanders, he had to present himself at the headquarters of the BdU [C.-in-C. U-boats] and render a personal account of his latest patrol. On the strength of his report, and of the entries in *U43*'s war diary, the BdU's staff were equally convinced that *U43* had on 3 March, 1943, sunk a ship of the *Dunedin Star* class.

Of the *Doggerbank* there was no trace. According to the schedule laid down by Naval Operations, she should have reached Bordeaux a long time ago. What had become of the auxiliary cruiser and her precious cargo?

Press reports and information received from agents based in foreign ports had yielded no news of her. Although there was an outside chance that the *Doggerbank* had been stopped and seized by an Allied warship, it was more probable that she had been sunk. If so, how and where had it happened? As yet, it occurred to no one that there might be a connection between the *Doggerbank*'s disappearance and the sinking reported by the commander of *U43*.

Schwantke was decorated with the Iron Cross First Class and promoted *Kapitänleutnant* [lieutenant senior grade].

A small cabin on the upper deck of the *Campoamor* had been set aside as a sick-room. It was hot and stuffy, and the castaway was lying on the narrow bunk naked except for the dressings that covered the worst of his cuts and sores.

Captain Joaquin Diaz had been standing beside the bunk for some time. The man was restless. Unintelligible sounds issued from his swollen lips as he tossed and turned.

He had wasted away to a skeleton. Carducho had counted twenty-six notches on the dinghy's gunwale. Incredible, with no food or water on board. There was a strong possibility that they had rescued the man only to have him die on their hands.

'Has he drunk anything?' Diaz asked.

Carducho, who had been keeping watch over the castaway

since picking him up, shook his head. 'Nothing to speak of. The trouble is, he can't keep anything down. I tried spooning some broth into him, but he brought it all up.'

Diaz stared at the tattoos on the man's arms. They were oozing where the salt had eaten into them. 'I'll send out another SOS,' he said.

The *Campoamor*'s crew was too small to warrant a ship's doctor. As soon as the castaway had been picked up the tanker's radio operator had sent out an 'SOS – sick man on board', and a number of ships carrying doctors had replied. The *Campoamor* had reported the castaway's condition and received medical advice.

Diaz was puzzled. Carducho had found the man's name and nationality – German – carved into the boat's timbers, but how had he got there? German ships avoided these latitudes, which were heavily patrolled by the US Navy. There were one or two German submarines around, but the dinghy could hardly have come from a U-boat.

The unconscious man's lips were moving. Diaz bent over him, but all he could distinguish was '*Wasser*'.

'Maybe you should try him with plain water,' Diaz said. 'A spoonful of water with a few drops of brandy or rum in it.'

'It would burn his throat, Captain. Besides, the doctors said no alcohol. Perhaps we should dilute the broth some more.'

'Stay with him, anyway. I'll get someone to stand in for you.'

Their voices had brought him round. His vision was blurred. He could see no one at first, just shadows. Then he heard men speaking a foreign language. Red-yellow-red . . . had he really seen a Spanish flag?

He tried to sit up, but it was hopeless, so he lay still. Where was he? Still in the dinghy – still under the sail? It was as hot and stuffy as it had been there, but he wasn't lying on bare wood. This was a softer surface.

He explored it with his hands. It felt like cloth, like a cotton sheet. And then he noticed the motion: no, that wasn't the gentle rocking of the dinghy.

A ship! The thought flashed through his mind. That faint vibration, that muffled pounding, could only be made by the engines of a ship under way. What a sound! It was the sweetest he'd ever heard.

He must have dozed off. It was dark when he awoke, but the sound was still there; he hadn't been mistaken. The voices had ceased, but someone was sitting beside him. He turned his head and saw a giant of a man; a man he'd seen before. In the dinghy? The big man was sitting up straight. His shirt was open at the neck, and when he leant forwards, as he did now, Kuert saw a lucky charm dangling from a gold chain.

He felt a hand slide beneath his head and raise it, felt the rim of a mug being gently insinuated between his lips. He could smell beef broth. He remembered now: they had tried to get some down him before, but he had brought it up. Why broth, for God's sake? Where was his canteen of rum? A sip of rum was all he wanted, but he couldn't say so. He pointed to his lips.

The man bending over him looked mystified and concerned. What was the Spanish for rum? Surely this big fellow should have got the message by now?

Then he drifted off again.

This time it was the smell of rum that brought him round.

You're dreaming, he told himself, but it persisted: the unmistakable smell of brown rum. A light was burning in the cabin; yes, it was a cabin. The Spaniard wearing the lucky charm was seated beside his bunk with a bottle of rum and a tumbler with a spoon in it. Kuert was thirstier than ever, thirstier than on any day in the dinghy. If he'd had the strength he would have snatched the bottle from the Spaniard's hand. What was he waiting for? Why was he looking so worried? *Rum, give me some rum!*

He watched the Spaniard pour some into the tumbler; barely enough to cover the bottom; and half fill the glass with water. One hand helped him to sit up, the other raised the glass to his lips.

He reached for it avidly, scared that it might be removed

at the last moment. Even the touch of the glass on his lips hurt like hell, but he drank, swallowed, and gave an almost simultaneous croak of pain. The rum burned his throat like fire, burned his stomach as well. He writhed and moaned, but he didn't vomit.

Mehr, more. Why in God's name had he never learnt Spanish? *More.* But the big man tried him with broth again. The very smell of it nauseated him. He drank some and promptly brought it up, along with that lovely rum, he thought sadly.

I've got to get at that bottle.

He lay there, half-asleep but obsessed with the thought. Then he noticed that he was alone. *The rum bottle.* He'd seen where the Spaniard had put it, in a kind of medicine chest. How to get at it, though? He tried to sit up, but without success. Rolling to the edge of the bunk, which wasn't very far from the ground, he fell off and landed with a crash. He lay there for a moment, gathering his strength. Then, ears pricked for any sound of footsteps outside, he crawled to the cupboard on all fours.

He opened the cupboard and picked up the bottle in both hands, barely able to support its weight. He noticed the state of his hands for the first time. He unscrewed the cap. The smell of the rum brought him to his senses. Did he know what he was doing? He was scared of the pain, the searing pain, but some overriding instinct told him that the spirit would restore him, cleanse him, as long as he didn't drink too much. Just a mouthful, no more.

He drank. The pain was unendurable, but once again he didn't vomit. The bottle slipped through his fingers. All at once he felt infinitely weary, but it was a pleasant, soothing sensation. There was the vibration, too. He could feel it even more distinctly, lying on the floor. The engine-room must be situated beneath him, and the steady, unvarying rhythm of the engines was like a heartbeat: boo-boom, boo-boom, boo-boom. He wasn't sure which he was hearing, the ship or his heart.

They found Kuert on the floor with the bottle beside him,

picked him up and put him back in his bunk. Then he slept soundly, without stirring or talking in his sleep, for twenty hours, twenty solid hours during which they could hardly tell if he was still breathing.

His aches and pains smote him with full intensity when he awoke, but his mind was quite clear. He learned the ship's name and its destination: Aruba.

He drank a cup of beef broth, and this time he kept it down. He was too weak to stand or walk unaided, but he managed a few steps with the help of the boatswain and a steward.

There were some bathroom scales in his cabin. Supported by the two men, he weighed himself. In normal times he weighed 180 pounds; now he was down to 80. He stared at the dial uncomprehendingly. His worst moment came when he caught sight of himself in the mirror on the inside of the locker door, a skeletal figure covered in sores. He looked at the figure without at first recognizing it as his own.

The face was hollow-eyed and spectral, the once broad shoulders drooped, the collar-bones protruded. The entire body was leprous with cuts and sores, and the skin, even when unbroken, was as scaly as a herring's.

At no time in the dinghy had he felt as wretched and helpless as he did now, in front of that mirror. He would never pull through, he told himself. He would never get back on his legs. He began to weep uncontrollably. His body shook like that of a man in a fever as the other two helped him back to his bunk.

They sighted Aruba two days later, on 1 April. At noon the *Campoamor* stopped engines and anchored in the roads outside the oil port of Oranjestad. The castaway had been installed in a reclining chair on deck, where he lay swathed in blankets despite the heat. Too weak to walk unaided, he had been helped on deck and over to the chair by Carducho and another man. His diet was still limited to mugs of watery broth and spoonfuls of diluted rum. He was wearing a shirt and trousers borrowed from the youngest ship's boy, but even those were too big for him.

Kuert could see the port from his vantage-point on deck. Aruba. The island's name had rung a bell the first time he heard it, but until now he hadn't been able to remember why. It was hard to collect his thoughts. They were dominated day and night by his experiences since the sinking of the *Doggerbank*; anything prior to that seemed shrouded in a kind of mist.

A boat emerged from the harbour and headed for the *Campoamor* in a wide arc. It was a pilot boat flying the Dutch flag.

He had a sense of *déjà vu*. There was something familiar about the scene. Aruba. Then he remembered: he'd been here before, two or three times at least, but when? Before the war, certainly. With a ship, naturally. The MTS *Brake*, a tanker. They had taken on oil here, like the Spaniard. It must have been in 1936 or 1937, before the war anyway. He couldn't have been more than eighteen or nineteen, a sturdy young seaman, not the pathetic wreck he was now. Yet again, he felt tears of weakness spring to his eyes.

The pilot boat was now claiming all his attention. He watched it until the ship hid it from view. Then he transferred his gaze to the place where the pilot would come aboard. The pilot soon appeared, but he wasn't alone. Following him were three men in US Navy uniform. One was an officer, the other two wore MP arm-bands and carried submachine guns. They disappeared in the direction of the captain's cabin.

Kuert looked at Carducho, who was standing nearby. The Spanish boatswain shrugged his shoulders to convey that this was quite normal: the island of Aruba was neutral territory, but the Americans, who maintained a substantial base there, ruled the roost.

'You won't hand me over, will you?'

The boatswain gave another shrug.

'The captain promised he'd take me back to Spain.'

Kuert had been counting on it, though the prospect of an Atlantic crossing in the *Campoamor* filled him with dread. She was a neutral vessel, but even neutral vessels could be sunk. At some stage he had vowed never to set foot in another ship, but his desire to return to Germany was too strong. *I've got to go back*. The thought obsessed him. It had to do with the sinking of the *Doggerbank* and the submarine that had sent her to the bottom.

The captain of the *Campoamor* had questioned him about it, naturally. Carducho and the signal officer, who both spoke a smattering of German, had taken him to Captain Diaz as soon as he was making sense. He vaguely remembered the form the interrogation had taken. What was the name of his ship? The *Doggerbank*. Outward bound from where? Japan. Her cargo? Crude rubber, for the most part. Where had she been sunk? Approximately 36 degrees north, 34 west. That was over 1600 miles away! Could he indicate the place on the map? He remembered how his fingers had trembled as he pointed to a spot south-west of the Azores. How had the ship been sunk? Torpedoed.

Joaquin Diaz had accepted the last answer without querying the nationality of the submarine. After all, why should he? The idea that it might have been a U-boat was far too monstrous to entertain. Even he, Kuert, was beginning to have his doubts. It didn't matter anyway, not right now. It could wait until he got back

'He promised I could stay aboard.'

'Of course,' said Carducho.

Kuert had a sudden thought. 'Did he send off a signal about me?'

'Yes. An SOS, because we don't carry a doctor.'

'Anything else?'

'He said we'd picked you up, and so on.'

'My nationality?'

'It's customary.'

'And the name of my ship? The place where she went down?'

'Possibly, but that's customary too. What else could we do? We're a neutral ship.'

Of course! That explained the presence of the Americans. They'd now been in the captain's cabin for a good half-hour. Kuert could imagine what that meant. A German sailor.

Heaven alone knew what secrets the Americans hoped to extract from him.

A seaman appeared at Kuert's elbow: Captain Diaz would like a word with him. Carducho and the seaman helped him to the captain's cabin. The two naval MPs were standing guard outside. As soon as he entered he could tell from the captain's face that his suspicions were well founded.

The American officer, it transpired, was a doctor. He barely glanced at Kuert, then turned to Diaz. 'You can't possibly keep this man on board, he's in very bad shape. He needs proper medical treatment in a hospital ashore. He could die on you. Are you prepared to take that responsibility? Think it over. I'll be back in an hour.'

Joaquin Diaz didn't speak for a while after the American had left the cabin. 'Perhaps it really would be best,' he said at length, 'for your own sake.'

'But I'm doing all right.'

'They can force my hand. We're a neutral ship, of course, but they'll make difficulties. They won't let us take on oil. They won't provision us or give us any drinking water or fuel. There are plenty of options open to them.'

He wasn't just making empty excuses, Kuert could tell. 'You mean they've asked you to hand me over?'

'More or less, yes.'

The crew of the *Campoamor* had picked him up, saved his life. If it hadn't been for them . . . He might have survived in the dinghy for another couple of days, he estimated. By then he might possibly have drifted with the current to one of the many small islands in the Lesser Antilles, Antigua, perhaps, or Guadeloupe or Dominica, but the British were firmly installed on most of them and the French on the rest. Schneidewind's original decision might have been the right one, but Schneidewind was dead. Not even Papa Boywitt, who had stuck it out with him for so long, had survived. He alone was alive.

I'm alive, what else matters? He started to weep again. His knees buckled, and he would have collapsed if they hadn't caught him in time. It didn't really matter what became of him. He was weary, infinitely weary. Even as he stood there, he felt himself falling asleep on his feet.

He was roused by the sound of a siren. For a moment he thought he was in an ambulance, but he saw when he opened his eyes that he was still on board ship and back in his bunk. Carducho and the signal officer were there. Audible through the open porthole, the wail of the siren grew louder, then died away.

'The Americans?'

Carducho nodded.

He was ready. He had no need to pack; all he possessed was a borrowed pair of trousers, a borrowed shirt and his life. For the first time, he thought to inquire about the dinghy.

'What became of the boat? The boat you found me in?'

'We set it adrift.'

What had there been in the dinghy? He could only remember the knife and the guns. Had Carducho taken them as souvenirs? He wanted to ask but refrained. They would only have been perpetual reminders of things best forgotten.

Once on deck, he saw that the ship had now berthed. Parked on the quayside was an olive-green van adorned with a red cross on a white ground. Flanking it were two jeeps, and standing beside them were four armed US marines. And all, thought Kuert, for the sake of one feeble, exhausted German seaman.

Captain Diaz was waiting for him at the head of the accommodation ladder. Most of the tanker's crew were there too, just as they had been when he was hoisted aboard in the net three days earlier. They stepped aside as the captain came up to Kuert and kissed him on both cheeks.

Two medical orderlies were ready with a stretcher on the quayside below. He wanted to make his way to the ambulance unaided and unescorted, but then he saw the crowd that had gathered around the little American convoy. The hatred in the bystanders' faces puzzled him until he heard scattered cries in Dutch. 'Nazi!' he heard. 'Death to Hitler!' His American escorts held their guns at the ready.

He didn't resist when they lifted him on to the stretcher. It was only a few steps to the ambulance, but the rocking motion made him feel sick and dizzy. He shut his eyes as they slid him into the interior. When he opened them again he saw a dark wall of metal towering over him: a ship's side, portholes, a red-and-yellow flag. It had all happened once before.

The doors closed, enveloping him in gloom, and the ambulance set off. His sickness and dizziness returned. That rocking motion. Where was he? Then the siren started wailing and his mind cleared: Aruba, an American ambulance, two jeeps. What a performance! He almost felt like laughing, but he didn't delude himself: he might be bound for a hospital bed, but he was, to all intents and purposes, a prisoner of war.

An enciphered radio message from Spain broke the news. It was only a routine report from the naval attaché at the German embassy in Madrid, but it enabled the German Admiralty to solve the mystery of the *Doggerbank*.

According to the signal from Madrid, which was simultaneously picked up and deciphered without difficulty by the British, a Captain Joaquin Diaz had made the following deposition on his return from a voyage to Venezuela:

Three days before reaching her destination, the island of Aruba, the *Campoamor* had picked up a castaway adrift in a dinghy. The man had given his particulars as Boatswain Fritz Kuert of the German merchant marine, last ship the *Doggerbank*. On 3 March of the same year, south-west of the Azores at a spot some 36 degrees north, 34 west, his ship had been sunk by a submarine. The Dutch and US authorities at Aruba had requested that the said Kuert be turned over to them, and their request had been granted.

The report reached Berlin, where it was evaluated by Abteilung Seekrieg I, or ISKL, the department to which responsibility for all German merchantmen and auxiliary cruisers had been assigned for the duration of the war.

Late in 1942 ISKL had launched a major blockade-running operation which would, it was hoped, transport a total of 140,000 tons of dry goods and 70,000 tons of vegetable oils to Germany from the Far East. The *Doggerbank* was one of the vessels engaged in this operation and one of the first to be expected back from her long and circuitous voyage. She was thus a particularly valuable ship, not only on account of her cargo, but also because her captain's debriefing report promised to be highly informative. In the event, the *Doggerbank* never reached Bordeaux, her port of destination.

The staff officers at ISKL had been debating the *Doggerbank*'s whereabouts for weeks. The signal from Madrid disposed of that question, but it failed to reveal exactly what had happened. Kuert, it was quickly ascertained, had been a member of the *Doggerbank*'s crew. The sea area where she had been sunk was regarded as exceptionally dangerous, being situated in the narrowest part of the Atlantic and the one most vulnerable to enemy surveillance. As for the date of the sinking, 3 March, 1943, the German Admiralty found this puzzling because the *Doggerbank* was not assumed to have made such good progress. Most puzzling of all, however, was the report that she had been sunk by a submarine.

No enemy submarine had claimed a sinking on that day, and the enemy would scarcely have neglected to report such a success. Inquiries were made at Section OP, Operation Atlantic, of IISKL.

A check was run on the records at HQ C.-in-C. U-Boats, situated in the Hotel am Steinplatz, Berlin-Charlottenburg. A sinking on 3 March, 1943, south-west of the Azores? The war diaries, or logs, of Germany's own submarines were examined as a matter of routine. Had any U-boat reported such a sinking?

Only one had done so: *U43*, commanded by the newly-promoted *Kapitänleutnant* Hans-Joachim Schwantke. However, Schwantke had reported sinking a British ship. More than that, he had come to Berlin for debriefing in the regulation manner. It was customary for A5, the staff officer responsible for recording and confirming all 'kills', to ask U-boat captains awkward questions and make them pore over ships' silhouettes. Schwantke claimed to have sunk the *Dunedin Star*, or at least a ship of the same class, and his claim was finally confirmed.

But now? For the first time, C.-in-C. U-boats' chief of staff began to have doubts. The *Dunedin Star* outweighed the *Doggerbank* by nearly 3000 tons. Could Schwantke's estimate have been so wide of the mark? The date of the sinking, as reported by the captain of *U43*, was identical with that cited by the *Doggerbank*'s sole survivor. The same applied to the ship's position when sunk. Wasn't this one coincidence too many? The castaway was unavailable for questioning. Where was Schwantke, out on patrol again? No, still on leave.

Schwantke was summoned back to Berlin, together with all members of his crew who had been on the *U43*'s bridge when it surfaced after the attack. By now it was May, 1943, or over two months since the *Doggerbank* went down.

The experienced and highly decorated naval officers assigned to the board of inquiry, all of them former U-boat commanders, soon ascertained the truth. They found after renewed questioning 'that *U43* had, in fact, sunk the *Doggerbank*. The captain's evaluation of her class and size was very inaccurate, with the result that his war diary entries could not at first be reconciled with the *Doggerbank*.'

In view of these facts, should the captain of *U43* be court-martialled? The question was carefully debated in consultation with ISKL. Was Schwantke guilty, and if so of what? No one had warned him to look out for a blockade-runner. He had violated no ban on attacking lone merchantmen, nor had he broken any regulation by failing to pick up survivors, even though this might have enabled him to rescue a considerable proportion of the *Doggerbank*'s crew.

But there was yet another consideration. At this stage of the war, when German U-boat commanders were putting to sea in obsolete, ill-equipped boats, patrolling the Atlantic was a form of living hell. The heavy losses incurred by the U-boat arm necessitated that Schwantke reassume command of *U43*. This being so, it would be preferable not to burden him with the information that he had sunk a German ship.

Such was the conclusion reached by *Fregattenkapitän* [Commander] Günther Hessler, one of the staff officers who participated in the inquiry: 'We all knew how the men felt when they went out on patrol, and how much they had to contend with, so we never did anything that might add to a captain's mental burdens by raising disciplinary matters before he put to sea. The information that he [Schwantke] had sunk the *Doggerbank* could not have failed to impose an immense psychological strain. The realization that he had sunk one of our own ships would have hit him hard.'

So the file on the sinking of the *Doggerbank* remained closed. Relatives of her 364 dead who inquired after their menfolk received the following brief communication: 'Precise details cannot and must not be divulged for reasons of security. We are at war, and any information that may imperil ships or their crews must be withheld.'

Schwantke, now promoted *Kapitänleutnant*, had returned to Lorient to make his boat ready for sea. *U43* departed its base on 13 July, 1943.

We shall never know for certain if Schwantke was really as ignorant of the *Doggerbank*'s true nationality as C.-in-C. U-Boats' staff officers hoped and assumed. Wouldn't his misgivings have been aroused by the recall to Berlin and the renewed interrogation, not only of himself but of members of his crew as well? Whatever the truth, one eye-witness claims that he was unusually moody, withdrawn and uncommunicative in the days immediately preceding his departure on patrol.

Schwantke did not receive his full orders until he was at sea. He was instructed by radio to proceed to West Africa and mine the waters off the Nigerian port of Lagos, a major Allied trans-shipment point.

It was quite coincidental, nothing more, that *U43*'s prescribed route should have taken it almost exactly over the *Doggerbank*'s last resting-place at the bottom of the Atlantic.

The sky above Aruba was radiantly blue on 13 July, 1943. Twenty-odd people were standing outside the hangar in the hot summer sunlight, waiting for the US Navy plane to complete its preparations for take-off. A few of them were servicemen going on leave – they would fly to Havana and from there to the mainland – but the majority were sick men in need of more elaborate medical treatment than the rough-and-ready US hospital on Aruba could provide. Standing a little apart from the rest were a doctor and the only civilian in the party. The most noticeable thing about the latter was the condition of his face and hands, which were a mass of peeling skin.

Fritz Kuert, the castaway from the *Doggerbank*, had been an American prisoner in the Netherlands Antilles for nearly three-and-a-half months. His state of health was still poor, which was partly why it had been decided to transfer him to a hospital in New Orleans.

His condition for the first few days after being picked up was relatively good, all things considered, but it hadn't lasted. He suffered a relapse and developed pneumonia into the bargain. His sea-water sores, which refused to heal, continuously oozed and suppurated. His heart and his immune system had been weakened.

It was six weeks before he could walk unaided, and he was slow to put on weight in spite of ample food and regular vitamin injections. They'd weighed him yet again that morning: he now tipped the scales at 120 pounds, or 60 pounds less than his weight before the sinking. Even now, under the hot July sun, he was shivering like a man with malaria.

He saw the aircraft taxi out on to the apron. It looked very small, and he couldn't help reflecting that their flight would take them over water all the way. He glimpsed the sea, blue and sparkling, at the end of the runway.

'Nervous?' The American doctor smiled at him. 'You wanted it this way.'

The doctor was right. Kuert had been informed a week ago that he was to be transferred to the States by sea, in a troopship already berthed in the harbour. He had refused. He had even threatened to kill himself rather than set foot in another ship.

His vehemence had surprised him. He was a seaman through and through. He loved the sea and had always felt safe afloat, confident that nothing dire could ever happen to him and that, even if it did, he would survive. Survive he had, but he knew he could never summon up the strength to do so a second time. Besides, there were U-boats around.

The Caribbean, through which US tankers had to pass on their way to the oil ports of Venezuela and Mexico, was a hunting-ground much favoured by U-boat commanders, who willingly made the long trans-Atlantic voyage for a chance to attack the US tanker fleets. Aruba and Kuert's hospital were alive with rumours – terrifying reports that German submarines had sunk more tankers in a single day than were listed in Lloyd's Register. The truth was less dramatic. A U-boat had attacked a tanker anchored in the roads. The torpedoes missed, exploded against a quay, and killed a dozen dockers.

The island had been a hotbed of U-boat horror stories ever since. Fishermen claimed to have spotted periscopes, coastguards told of U-boats landing spies by night. The great U-boat panic was another reason for Kuert's transfer to the States. The *Campoamor*'s castaway was not entirely trusted. Could his story be a fabrication?

Had he really been the boatswain of the *Doggerbank*? Had he really spent twenty-six days sailing an open boat 1600 miles across the Atlantic? What if he were a German submariner, perhaps even the captain of a U-boat that had come to grief? Wasn't he always raving about a U-boat in his feverish dreams? If there was more to the matter than met the eye, it would be better to interrogate him in the States. And that was how he came to be boarding a plane on 13 July.

The sick were escorted to the waiting Dakota by a uniformed nurse. The concrete runway and the plane's metal fuselage shimmered in the sunlight. A minute earlier Kuert had been shivering; now he broke out in a sweat, so overwhelmed by heat that he felt he was in a Turkish bath. Everything had seemed so simple on board the *Campoamor*: he had been rescued, he was alive, he would pull through. The horrific mental images would fade, he had told himself. Now, as the plane took off and the sea slid into view below him, a wide blue expanse of watered silk, he knew he was wrong: they would remain with him for the rest of his days.

U43 was now in mid Atlantic. The outward voyage across the Bay of Biscay had been as arduous as usual. Enemy aircraft patrolled the area unceasingly, and *U43* could only proceed on the surface by night.

On 30 July, seventeen days after leaving Lorient, *Kapitän-leutnant* Schwantke's boat reached the sea area south-west of the Azores where it had sunk the *Doggerbank* on 3 March.

The weather was fine and sunny, as it had been then. That morning *U43* had rendezvoused with *U403*. In addition to mines for the Lagos operation, *U43* was carrying extra fuel to enable it to act as a 'milch cow', or submarine tanker, and some of this was pumped across to *U403*.

The sun was nearing its zenith. The two submarines rode the long, sluggish swell side by side.

Once *U403* had taken on oil for its diesel engines, the two captains exchanged a final salute. Then *U43* cast off and got under way.

The lookouts were at their posts. The sea was calm and deserted, but appearances were deceptive: *U43* and *U403* had already been spotted. An enemy aircraft, a Wildcat from VC29 Squadron, had detected both U-boats with its new short-wave D/F equipment. It had taken off from the US aircraft carrier *Santee*, which was proceeding westwards with Convoy GUS 10.

The Wildcat, up-sun from the U-boats and a considerable distance away, escaped detection by their lookouts. The pilot had radioed the *Santee*, which promptly dispatched two

Avenger bombers. The Avengers were duly guided to their quarry by the Wildcat.

The Wildcat made the first pass. It dived on the U-boats out of the dazzling sun. The pilot saw figures running to man the guns, but they never got there. Machine-gun bullets slammed into the casing and whipped the sea into a lather, mowing down the gun crews like a scythe. As he pulled out, the pilot saw those who were still alive running back to the conning tower.

Both submarines proceeded to dive. *U403* was quicker off the mark, either because its commander, *Kapitänleutnant* Heine, had spotted the aircraft sooner, or because his boat was lighter and more manoeuvrable without the cargo of mines carried by *U43*. Whatever the reason, *U403* had already submerged by the time the two Avengers dived in line-ahead like a pair of squat, snub-nosed bullets.

U403 escaped with minor damage, but it escaped, for the time being. One week later, having been hunted without respite, it was cornered and sunk. Not so *U43*, Schwantke's boat.

The second Avenger, piloted by USN Lieutenant Robert F. Richmond, was still two hundred metres from the U-boat, which had begun to submerge. The fore-casing was already awash when the Avenger released its pair of bombs and a 'Tido', or homing torpedo.

Richmond pulled out and observed the submarine through his side window.

What happened next was so unexpected, so terrible a spectacle, that he couldn't at first account for it.

U43 blew up like a gigantic firework, debris flew in all directions, flames shot into the air.

The series of explosions went on and on. The turbulence was so extreme that Richmond was hard put to it to keep his Avenger airborne. When he flew over the spot a minute later, nothing could be seen but a big, spreading patch of oil.

The truth dawned on him at last: mines!

The U-boat must have been carrying mines; it was, in effect, a floating ammunition dump.

The date was 30 July, 1943. *U43* and its crew had survived the men of the *Doggerbank* by less than five months.

And this time there was no survivor to tell the tale.

In New Orleans the *Doggerbank*'s sole survivor had suffered a relapse and was lying in the isolation ward of the military hospital, stricken with typhus. His condition remained grave for three months, then improved. He was transferred to Interrogation Camp No. 6, a secret facility, also known as 'Meade', that formed part of the Fort George prisoner-of-war camp. The curious thing was, Meade's personnel specialized in the interrogation of German submarine crews. The suspicion that Kuert was a U-boat man clung to him like a bur, so much so that the camp authorities issued him with German submariner's clothing. He was grilled by the Americans and British in turn, but he stuck to his story. Then, in October, the interrogations suddenly ceased. It was clear that his story had been corroborated by information received from other sources: the *Doggerbank*, alias Ship 52, formerly the *Speybank*, had been sunk by a German submarine! For Boatswain Fritz Kuert, this was his first confirmation of a fact he had always thrust to the back of his mind.

His next ports of call were Fort Myers and the hospital at Valley Forge. Then, midway through December 1943, he was informed that his name appeared on the latest list of prisoners earmarked for exchange. Who in Germany had put him on it? Who considered him, a humble boatswain, important enough to be released?

Just before the turn of the year he boarded the *Charles A. Stafford*, a ship on charter to the International Red Cross. Her port of destination was Marseilles. From there he and the others would travel by train to Geneva to be exchanged for American prisoners of war. Then Germany. That was where he would finally learn the whole truth, but to what end? What would it avail him? More particularly, what would it avail

147

his former shipmates? Schneidewind, Stachnovski, Bahrend, Waldemar, Papa Boywitt – all the others were dead. Much time had gone by, and time was said to be a healer, so what motivated him? Simply the thought that he was the *Doggerbank*'s sole survivor, and that he alone could ascertain the truth on the others' behalf.

That thought was uppermost in his mind throughout the crossing.

That and fear. The neutral ship was brightly illuminated, but it was still wartime. Despite the cold, he spent the days and nights on deck, never leaving the vicinity of the lifeboats. And, just as Jan Bahrend used to do, he kept a weather eye open for submarines.

EPILOGUE

Kuert waited out the end of the war in his Hamburg hiding-place. There were no ships in which he could have sailed, even had he wanted to, so he returned to his parental home and obtained a job at the colliery where his father worked, a job above ground though, because his state of health precluded anything more strenuous. He helped to rebuild his parents' bomb-damaged house, got married, and fathered three children. He had survived.

But then came the letters. From Papa Boywitt's wife, Schneidewind's family, Stachnovski's mother, Binder's sisters . . . Having learned that one member of the *Doggerbank*'s crew was alive, they begged him for information, for the truth that had never come out. He wrote back. His memories revived, and so did his urge to investigate anew. He tried to locate Schwantke and discovered that the captain of *U43* had survived his victims by only a few months. So why? What was he doing here?

A November day in 1961. More than eighteen years have passed since the *Doggerbank* went down.

He has an appointment in Aumühle, on the outskirts of Hamburg. A road lined with imposing suburban mansions, one of them being Dora Specht Allee 1. It sounds like an encoded U-boat signal, and the man who inhabits it was formerly, at various times, C.-in-C. U-Boats, Commander-in-Chief of the German Navy, and the Greater German Reich's last head of government: Grand Admiral Karl Dönitz.

It's eleven a.m. Fritz Kuert, erstwhile boatswain of the *Doggerbank*, is on time, but he hesitates briefly. What is he doing here, over eighteen years after the event?

Dönitz, an affable, white-haired old gentleman, answers the door in person and conducts him to the drawing-room. Before Kuert can say a word, he brings out a scrapbook filled with press cuttings. The *Doggerbank*? No, Nuremberg, his trial for war crimes, his years in Spandau Prison. He speaks of the cruel injustice he suffered at the hands of the Allies.

Kuert listens, looks at him, and wonders why he came. All the questions he has been meaning to ask seem pointless, now that he's face to face with this man who talks only of himself, of the wrongs and false accusations that *he* has had to endure.

The former grand admiral and the former boatswain sit facing each other in the drawing-room, which overlooks an immaculate garden.

'It's about the *Doggerbank*,' says Kuert. That, after all, is the reason for his presence.

Dönitz shakes his head. Heavens, it's so long ago. Of course he remembers the incident, naturally he does. A 'distressing business', but it was wartime, don't forget, and 'you can't make an omelette without breaking eggs . . .'

Listening to him, Kuert is struck by the realization that they're talking about entirely different things.

Three hundred and sixty-four men died a miserable, avoidable death, but their only memorial is a number, a small and insignificant item in the war's great balance sheet.

'We'd probably have court-martialled them, Schneidewind and Schwantke, and acquitted them both. A regrettable combination of circumstances.'

It's pointless to linger, pointless to listen to him any longer.

The two men rise. Dönitz, with a relieved smile, goes over to a writing desk and produces a postcard-sized photograph.

'I've only a few of these left.'

An official photograph from the great days of the Third Reich: Dönitz in his grand admiral's uniform, complete with orders and decorations.

He unscrews a fountain pen, scribbles a dedication: 'To Fritz Kuert in kind remembrance, Aumühle, 17 November, 1961.' Then he signs it.

Kuert takes the photograph.

In kind remembrance . . .

What he feels, for the very first time, is hatred, burning hatred for those who sacrificed the lives of his shipmates to no purpose, and mingled with that emotion is a sense of utter hopelessness.

He takes his leave.

It has started to rain. He walks off down the road, which is plastered with wet leaves. He doesn't look back.

He waits at the station. He has two more appointments scheduled for today, both with retired admirals, but he decides not to keep them.

The train pulls in. He boards it. He knows he won't ask any more questions, but he also knows he'll never be free of being the sole survivor of the *Doggerbank*.

DOCUMENTS

The foregoing account is based largely on statements obtained from the *Doggerbank*'s sole survivor, Fritz Kuert. These exist in the form of ten one-hour tape-recordings made in 1961 and numbered I-XX.

The Spanish captain's deposition dates from 1949, that of Captain Krage from 1961. The statement supplied by *Fregattenkapitän* [Commander] Hessler (ret.) also dates from the latter year, since when no new information about the sinking of the *Doggerbank* has come to light.

At the time of writing, more than thirty years after the ship went down, no purpose can be served by apportioning blame for the incident. Few, however, would disagree with Captain Krage's contention that the sinking of the *Doggerbank* was prompted by 'an unbridled destructive urge almost without parallel in the history of the sea'.

Statement by Fregattenkapitän Günther Hessler, formerly on the staff of C.-in-C. U-boats.

It was quite clear that, if blockade-runners were to pass safely through the Atlantic, an area in which German submarines were operating, special precautions had to be taken to prevent those submarines from sinking them.

It was the practice of all Allied vessels crossing the Atlantic to 'darken ship', in other words, they sailed without showing the regulation lights and with portholes and scuttles blacked out. Thus, blockade-runners had also to darken ship, or they would have attracted Allied attention.

By day they steered a zigzag course, just as Allied vessels did in order to render an attacking U-boat's task more difficult. Since Allied aircraft patrolled the Atlantic, including the South Atlantic and the sea area south of Cape Town, any merchantman not steering a zigzag course would have attracted the attention of such aircraft. For that reason, German blockade-runners comported themselves neither more nor less suspiciously than any Allied vessel.

Until September, 1942, German submarines operated mainly in the North Atlantic and only to a very limited extent in the South Atlantic. From October, 1942, onwards they pushed south into the vicinity of Cape Town and, from the spring of 1943, into the Indian Ocean, with the result that those areas, too, became combat zones. One can readily understand why the safety regulations previously in force in the North Atlantic had then to be extended to the whole of the South Atlantic and the Indian Ocean.

When homeward bound, ordinary merchantmen or blockade-runners kept within an area prescribed by the German Admiralty. Code-named 'Weg Anton' [Route A], this corridor varied between three and four hundred nautical miles in width. It began in the North Atlantic, west of the Azores at a point some 30 degrees west, ran due south as far as possible from the African coast, cut more or less through the middle of the so-called 'narrows' between Freetown [Sierra Leone] and Natal [Brazil], and headed south-east to the Cape, which it rounded at a distance of some three hundred miles. Every blockade-runner's captain had a top secret chart showing 'Weg Anton' and maintained radio contact with ISKL [Section I of Naval Operations], which was responsible for all German merchantmen and auxiliary cruisers at sea. ISKL, in its turn, was in close touch with IISKL, or C.-in-C. U-boats. The latter was officially designated IISKL BdUOA, or 'Commander of Submarines, Operation Atlantic'.

The German Admiralty kept a running check on the position of every U-boat, so it always knew the whereabouts, not only of its operational submarines, but also of German blockade-runners and auxiliary cruisers. It knew how fast such vessels could travel when making the long homeward voyage of over 10,000 miles. Their captains received written orders at their ports of departure, which were enciphered and radioed to the German naval attaché in Tokyo. To the extent that these orders were incomplete, however, captains were advised while at sea what route they should follow and precisely when they should pass through particular stretches of 'Weg Anton'. The German Admiralty, which passed these instructions to blockade-runners by radio, did not in general expect them to be acknowledged because of the risk of detection by enemy D/F stations.

The British and Americans, who maintained D/F stations at many points on the Atlantic coast and throughout the Indian Ocean, were capable of accurately plotting a ship's position within minutes of picking up its signals. For that reason, blockade-runners avoided communicating with the German Admiralty by radio unless they had already been detected by the enemy or had some vital information to impart. They would alter course immediately after doing so, veering off in an unlikely direction in the hope of making it more difficult for the enemy to locate them with the aid of aircraft, warships, or auxiliary cruisers.

Instructions of this nature had been radioed to Captain Schneidewind. One such signal, sent on 14 February, 1943, ordered him not under any circumstances to cross the equator in a northerly direction until 5 March.

Schneidewind was still in the South Atlantic when he received this signal. This sea area was exposed to far less surveillance than the North Atlantic, so he could, if already too far north, have killed time there by reducing speed.

If Schneidewind had crossed the equator on 5 March, 12 March was the earliest date on which he could have reached the spot where his ship was, in fact, sunk on 3 March. It is possible, therefore, though we shall never know for sure, that he failed to pick up the relevant signal.

The German Admiralty's signals to blockade-runners in the Atlantic always made a special point of warning them to avoid areas in which U-boats were currently operating against Allied convoys. Every blockade-runner had either to bypass such areas or wait until the convoys and U-boats had vacated them. The efficiency of this system can be gauged from the fact that ships using 'Weg Anton' had hitherto reached France unscathed. To cite one example, the blockade-runner *Friedberg* had used 'Weg Anton' only a few days previously. On 24 February she was met by three German submarines some 150 miles north of the Azores island of Flores, at a rendezvous of which she had been advised by radio. The U-boats were to escort her to France, but in this case their protection proved ineffective. Two days later an Allied aircraft sighted the blockade-runner some 400 miles west of the Spanish coast. The pilot called up a British cruiser, which shot her to pieces at such long range that the U-boats could not mount an attack.

This incident does, nevertheless, demonstrate that the pre-arranged ban on attacking unescorted vessels had enabled the *Friedberg* to traverse the U-boat-infested area south of the Azores with complete success.

U43 returned to Lorient on 31 March, 1943. Like all U-boat captains, Schwantke had to submit a report on his latest patrol. At these interviews, which were held during April and May 1943 at the headquarters of C.-in-C. U-boats in Berlin-Charlottenburg, every U-boat captain had to present a detailed account of his experiences.

The meetings were usually chaired by Dönitz himself or by his chief of staff, Admiral Godt. If the latter was unavailable, I myself conducted the proceedings. As a rule, however, Dönitz presided.

The U-boat's war diary was closely examined, and questions were put by each of the staff officers present. After interviewing Schwantke, none of us was in any doubt that he had sunk a ship of the *Dunedin Star* class, possibly the *Dunedin Star* herself. It did not become clear to ISKL that the vessel in question might possibly have been the *Doggerbank* until

May/June 1943, after the potential causes of her disappearance had been carefully investigated.

This assumption was subsequently corroborated by a report from Spain that a Spanish ship had picked up a survivor from the *Doggerbank*, and that the survivor had stated that his ship had been torpedoed and sunk south of the Azores on 3 March.

Since no other sinking had occurred on that date, and since the silhouette described by *U43*'s captain roughly corresponded to that of the *Doggerbank*, the German Admiralty realized that she might have been the ship in question. After receiving information from abroad that a survivor from the *Doggerbank* had been picked up, we checked all the sinkings that had taken place in the relevant period and came to the conclusion that *U43* must indeed have sunk the *Doggerbank*. No blame attached to the captain, who had acted as anyone would have done in his place, not having received any orders to beware of blockade-runners. It was consequently decided, after joint discussions with ISKL, not to institute court-martial proceedings against him. He was not brought before a court martial because it was clear to all the authorities concerned that he was not at fault, and because he had to go out on patrol again. But it is understandable that Schwantke was not court-martialled for another reason as well. Immense demands were made, particularly on young captains, by operational patrols conducted at a time when German submarine warfare was foundering. Attacks on Allied shipping in the North Atlantic virtually ceased on 25 May, 1943, because that was the date on which our U-boats were ordered to return to base. We subsequently resumed operations in the South Atlantic in June/July, but only so as to fill in the time until new and better-equipped types of U-boats became available.

Thus, the captains who put to sea at this period – June 1943 – could expect a very hard time of it out in the Atlantic.

Captain Schneidewind, the skipper of the *Doggerbank*, had displayed such care and tactical skill when mining the Agulhas Bank on the outward voyage to Japan, despite being spotted on three occasions, that he was entrusted with another special assignment on the voyage back to Europe.

Although blockade-runners kept as far as possible to the middle of the South and Central Atlantic, and in 1942/3 could still traverse that area in relative safety, the passage through Biscay and past the Azores was becoming increasingly difficult. To the best of my recollection, the *Doggerbank* was the last ship expected in western France that winter season. She was to diverge from the normal route and proceed northwards on a course considerably further east. She would thus be impersonating one of the lone Allied vessels that plied between West Africa and the British Isles, which at this period travelled unescorted until they were on a level with Gibraltar, but often proceeded still further north without joining a convoy.

The *Doggerbank*, formerly the *Speybank*, belonged to a class of British vessels of which numerous similar examples sailed the Atlantic. Schneidewind's instructions were conveyed to him by several incoming radio messages during the voyage and after his departure from the Dutch East Indies. He could select his own route, but was advised to steer close to various Spanish territories at particularly hazardous points. The *Doggerbank* was notified in good time of the sea areas from which our own submarines were excluded on her account. As a rough guide, she was also informed of her position as plotted by the German Admiralty. Instructions not to cross the equator before a certain, specified date were radioed to her ten days in advance.

Boatswain Kuert's assertion that the *Doggerbank* was expecting a U-boat escort is wholly incorrect. Kuert could not have known this. It is also an abiding mystery how Captain Schneidewind could have entered a sea area cleared for U-boat operations so far ahead of time. He must have maintained a mean speed almost one knot faster than on the outward voyage, and he must also have had the benefit of favourable currents, or he could never have reached a point so far north. It seems that Schneidewind trusted to luck and disregarded his instructions not to cross the equator before a certain date because he discovered that he had already just crossed it in a northerly direction when the signal was received. I had my signals and my plot of the *Doggerbank*'s position carefully double-checked by IISKL, as I recall – because I felt I might be responsible for sending her to her doom. The findings of this investigation accorded with my own, so Schneidewind's conduct remains inexplicable, the more so since he could have radioed not only south of the equator but on a level with it, for it must have been obvious to him from my signals that I put him much further south. I find his failure to use his radio all the more incomprehensible because he sent a brief 'burst' requesting a missing radio message the night before his first mine-laying operation, so he clearly knew how to do this.

Nothing more was heard of the ship thereafter. No enemy report pointed to its destruction, nor did our own U-boat successes furnish any clue to an inadvertent sinking. The German Admiralty had a mystery on its hands. Many weeks later, nearly three months, as I recall – the German naval attaché in Spain forwarded a report from a Spanish captain who had, while bound for Venezuela, encountered several dead [sic] and one survivor adrift in a boat: the last and only trace of the *Doggerbank*. The survivor stated that the *Doggerbank* had, on the night of 3 March, 1943, been sunk by a German submarine. The survivor was currently being held in custody by the Allied authorities, so the German Admiralty was unable to obtain any further information from him.

The German Admiralty found the alleged position and date quite incredible, because they implied that the *Doggerbank* had not only made better time than on the outward voyage but had flatly disregarded a definite order not to cross the equator before a given date. Both eventualities seemed highly improbable. Despite this, C.-in-C. U-boats' staff examined the war diaries of all the U-boats that had reported successes at the time in question. These disclosed three sinkings that might have been identified with the *Doggerbank*, although the vessels were quite dissimilar in size.

When the captains were questioned, it emerged that *U43* had indeed sunk the *Doggerbank* at a spot almost exactly eleven days' steaming further north than the German Admiralty's plot of her position. The ship was sunk during darkness, and her class and size were badly misjudged by *U43*'s captain, with the result that the entries in his war diary could not at first be reconciled with the *Doggerbank*.

A brief note on the elucidation of the *Doggerbank*'s disappearance was later entered in the German Admiralty's war-diary.

All the particulars given above were recorded in the form of memorandums and kept in a file in my office at Navy High Command, where they were later completely destroyed by fire.

Statement volunteered by Captain Friedrich A. Krage, one-time skipper of the Ärmeland, Weserland, *and other blockade-runners.*

As a blockade-runner captain and skipper of the first ship assigned to run the gauntlet from Japan to Europe, I recall that, where this first breakthrough was concerned, the orders transmitted to me by the captain of the auxiliary cruiser *Orion* did not instruct me to traverse specific areas at absolutely specific times.

SKL [Naval Operations] twice sent me orders by radio. On the first occasion I was instructed to rendezvous with the naval tanker *Altmark*. (This order was so imprecise that I would have been justified in ignoring it. After wrestling with my conscience, however, I finally decided to head in the *Altmark*'s direction, and all went well.) I was unable to carry out the second order, which reached me near the Azores, because it, too, contained inconsistencies. I mention this to show how difficult it was to transmit orders in the early years of the war.

It should also be remembered that a vessel engaged on such a long voyage was exposed to a variety of untoward occurrences such as engine trouble, the need to take avoiding action, adverse wind and weather, et cetera, so strict adherence to times and places was quite impossible. Moreover, wireless messages could not be sent from the ship for reasons of security.

When leaving Japan on my first blockade-running trip I was given US $10,000 in case engine trouble compelled the ship to put in at a neutral port – a sign that SKL was allowing for all contingencies. It was not until *after* the *Doggerbank* incident that the authorities, having learnt their lesson, insisted on strict adherence to times and positions. Had SKL sufficiently impressed on Captain Schneidewind the danger of traversing certain sea areas too soon, the conscientious Schneidewind would never have diverged from the route and timing laid down. SKL must have known that any ship making so long a voyage is often unable to manoeuvre according to plan for technical reasons, as I have already said. To allow for this very contingency, therefore, blockade-runners and warships should have been issued with valid and binding recognition signals.

Where the *Doggerbank* was concerned, the U-boat must have been surprised to encounter an unescorted ship at this period (1943), since all Allied ships, at least in the North Atlantic, were then accustomed to travelling in convoy. It is hard to understand why the U-boat captain's suspicions were not aroused. 'That ship merits a closer look,' he should have said to himself. 'She has spotted us, but she's making no attempt to escape or steer a zigzag course. On the contrary, she's proceeding at slow speed and trying to establish contact with us.' Under those circumstances, no normally conscientious U-boat captain would have sunk the vessel before trying to solve the mystery and ascertain the nationality of a target behaving in so strange a manner. Given the prevailing weather conditions and the absence of enemy aircraft, this would have been relatively easy and devoid of danger to the U-boat. Furthermore, an experienced U-boat commander equipped with powerful binoculars would have been struck by the number of men on board the other vessel.

To anyone who correctly evaluates the factors listed above and professionally assesses the position of the two vessels at the time of the sinking, there can be only one conclusion: the U-boat captain was unequal to his job. He, and he alone, was responsible for the ensuing calamity.

SKL bears a share of the blame in that it clearly failed to impress the requisite instructions on the U-boat captain with sufficient force, or to warn him that a blockade-runner might be encountered even in prohibited grid squares.

Given that the *Doggerbank* was proceeding at half speed in calm seas, and that her undeviating course rendered her the easiest of targets, it is incomprehensible that *U43*'s captain should have thought it necessary to fire three torpedoes at his putative enemy, when one well-aimed shot would just as surely have sealed her fate. The latter course of action would have had the twofold advantage of conserving torpedoes and, because the ship would have foundered more slowly, of enabling her crew to launch all the lifeboats. In that event, no lives might have been lost.

Shouldn't the victor's conscience have pricked him when the *Doggerbank* went down in a mere eight minutes? Shouldn't the human emotions deep within him have prevailed? Even from a purely naval and political standpoint, wasn't it incumbent on him to pick up at least one survivor and ascertain the vessel's nationality? It wasn't pitch-dark when *U43* surfaced, and the three officers on deck could clearly see men in the water just as the latter, for their part, could make out the submarine as it slowly approached. Those men were mortally afraid and fighting for their lives, but their cries for help went unheard. Truly, this was a blatant disregard of the most basic of human emotions. Verging on criminal brutality, it displayed an unbridled destructive urge almost without parallel in the history of the sea.

Statement addressed to Fritz Kuert by Captain Joaquin Diaz, master of the Spanish tanker Campoamor.

Spanish ships bound for America at this period [1943] were instructed by the Spanish naval authorities, acting in consultation with the belligerent powers, to enter the Caribbean by way of the Martinique narrows, using a corridor beginning 500 miles from the American coast, or at 50° west, and bounded by the 15th and 16th parallels. We, the tanker *Campoamor*, owned by CAMPSA of Madrid, were in that corridor on our way to Aruba.

At 13.05 on 29 March, 1943, the officer then on watch sighted a boat at 15°31' north, 51°21' west.

We were able to ascertain that it was a small craft. There was a sail on board that caught the sunlight.

We continued to observe the boat, and at 13.40 I stopped engines. We discovered that there was someone alive on board. I gave orders that the man be hoisted aboard with the utmost care, using a net we carried. This net had been made when we were lying at anchor off the port of Govenas [Colombia] in the Golfo de Morrosquillo. We used it to catch fish in the roads, because we had to wait forty days for a cargo and were running short of food.

You [the castaway, Fritz Kuert] were taken to the sickbay. You had lost consciousness, and we were afraid you would die at any moment. I ordered the radio operator to send an emergency signal: 'SOS – sick man on board.' This appeal was answered by various Allied warships and one Spaniard. I chose the Spanish ship in the belief that you would be better served. The doctor on the *Cabo de Hornos* did, in fact, assist me. The case sounded hopeless, he said, but there was still a faint chance.

Your body was naked except for a pair of briefs and a shirt full of holes. You were covered in sores from head to foot. By following the doctor's radioed instructions, we managed to save you. You told me, when you regained consciousness, that your ship was named the *Doggerbank*. She had come from the Far East and was bound for Germany via the Cape. Near the Azores she was torpedoed by a submarine. You and twelve [sic] other members of the crew, including the captain, were able to escape in a dinghy that had remained intact.

Your ship, the *Doggerbank*, was an armed merchantman carrying strategic materials and crude rubber.

You had been in the small craft for two or three days when a violent storm blew up and overturned it. The captain, who had grasped the situation, outlined your predicament and pronounced it hopeless; there was no point in going on. Your companions asked the captain to shoot them, which he did. When only you and one other man were left, you said you still hoped to make it. The captain then shot himself, leaving you and the other man alone together. The other man died after 22 days, so you were the last one left alive.

We found 26 notches carved on the dinghy's stern seat, signifying that you had spent 26 days aboard. Also found in the boat were a pistol, a knife, and some bloodstains. We set the boat adrift. The pistol was thrown into the sea, the knife I kept.

According to your information, the captain had a wife and children and lived in Hamburg. You gave me the address. You told me you would probably have held out for another two or three days had we not turned up and rescued you. After installing you in the sick-bay I proceeded on my way. You regained consciousness as we were passing Martinique. I radioed the authorities at Aruba. Your condition was still critical, and you had to be admitted to hospital. During the days you spent on board you were fed only what the doctor had prescribed: small spoonfuls of water laced with a few drops of spirit. Clothes and toilet articles were given you aboard the *Campoamor*. The whole crew was concerned about you and earnestly hoped that you would make a full recovery.

When you landed in Aruba you were hospitalized and later transferred to the United States as a prisoner of war.